I0197863

Edward William Nelson, C. Hart (Clinton Hart) Merriam

Natural History of the Tres Marias Islands, Mexico

Edward William Nelson, C. Hart (Clinton Hart) Merriam

Natural History of the Tres Marias Islands, Mexico

ISBN/EAN: 9783743319844

Manufactured in Europe, USA, Canada, Australia, Japa

Cover: Foto ©ninafisch / pixelio.de

Manufactured and distributed by brebook publishing software
(www.brebook.com)

Edward William Nelson, C. Hart (Clinton Hart) Merriam

Natural History of the Tres Marias Islands, Mexico

LETTER OF TRANSMITTAL.

U. S. Department of Agriculture,
Division of Biological Survey,
Washington, D. C., January 25, 1899.

Sir: I have the honor to transmit herewith for publication as North American Fauna No. 14 a report by E. W. Nelson on the natural history of the Tres Marias Islands, Mexico. These islands are the largest off the west coast between Cape St. Lucas and the Isthmus of Panama, but have seldom been visited, and very little is known of their fauna or flora. For several years Mr. Nelson has had charge of the field work of the Biological Survey in Mexico, and in May, 1897, visited the Tres Marias. During the course of this visit he made a thorough collection of birds and mammals and also secured specimens of reptiles, fishes, mollusks, crustaceans, and plants, so that his report contains a fairly complete account of the natural history of the islands. In working up the material collected, Mr. Nelson has had the assistance of several well known naturalists in the United States National Museum and United States Fish Commission, who have prepared reports on special groups, as credited in detail on page 13.

Mention should be made also of the unfailing courtesy and interest of the Mexican Government in the investigations conducted by the Biological Survey in Mexico. Letters have been furnished by officials in the City of Mexico, and by the late Mexican minister in Washington, Señor Don Matias Romero, which greatly facilitated the work in various ways, and on the occasion of the visit to the Tres Marias enabled Mr. Nelson to borrow a large boat at San Blas and secure comfortable quarters on the islands.

Several attempts at agriculture have been made on the Tres Marias Islands, but the results have thus far been unsuccessful, owing to the dry climate and the scarcity of permanent water. Corn and beans have been grown on a small scale, but the crops suffer from the severe storms which occur at certain seasons. Experiments have been made with a view to utilizing the native species of agave for fiber and mescal, and the cultivation of cotton has also been tried without success. Recently it has been proposed to establish an American colony on one of the islands for the purpose of growing coffee, bananas, Australian

3

chestnuts, and date palms, and to engage in the manufacture of banana and chestnut flour. Such a scheme, Mr. Nelson tells me, could only result in failure, as the islands are entirely unsuited to growing these products. It therefore seems desirable to publish at once all the information in the possession of the Department, for the purpose of making it available to those who may be interested in the islands or their products.

Respectfully,

C. HART MERRIAM,
Chief, Biological Survey.

Hon. JAMES WILSON,
Secretary of Agriculture.

CONTENTS.

	Page.
General description of the Tres Marias Islands, Mexico. By E. W. Nelson....	7
Mammals of the Tres Marias Islands. By E. W. Nelson......................	15
Birds of the Tres Marias Islands. By E. W. Nelson	21
Reptiles of the Tres Marias Islands. By Leonhard Stejneger...............	63
Notes on Crustacea of the Tres Marias Islands. By Mary J. Rathbun........	73
Plants of the Tres Marias Islands. By J. N. Rose	77
Partial Bibliography of the Tres Marias Islands. By E. W. Nelson	93

ILLUSTRATIONS.

PLATE.

Map of the Tres Marias Islands... Frontispiece.

FIGURES.

	Page.
1. *Erythrina lanata* Rose	81
2. *Euphorbia nelsoni* Millspaugh	89

GENERAL DESCRIPTION OF THE TRES MARIAS ISLANDS, MEXICO.

By E. W. Nelson.

INTRODUCTION.

The Tres Marias islands are situated off the west coast of Mexico, about 65 miles west from the port of San Blas. These islands have been known since early in the history of the New World, and in 1532 were named Las Islas de la Magdalena by Diego de Mendoza. Many of the early explorers sailed about them, and Dampier states that they were familiar to the buccaneers who visited these shores. They are mentioned by several of the later voyagers, especially the English exploring expeditions which visited the west coast of Mexico in the first half of the present century. During all this time, however, they remained uninhabited and nothing definite was known or published concerning their character or products. It is said at San Blas that the first men who lived upon the islands were bandits, who took refuge there, and had a secure retreat from which they harried the mainland settlements for several years. Finally, the abundance of Spanish cedar became known, a settlement of woodcutters was established on Marie Madre, and this island has since been continuously inhabited.

Col. A. J. Grayson, a naturalist who lived for many years on the west coast of Mexico, was the first to publish any detailed information about the islands.[1] Most of this information is contained in the various papers embodying the results of his three trips to the Tres Marias in 1865, '66, and '67, published by himself, George N. Lawrence, and W. E. Bryant. In 1881 Alphonse Forrer, a natural history collector, spent some time on Maria Madre collecting specimens for the British Museum, but no detailed account of his work has been published. No other naturalist is known to have visited the islands until the spring of 1897. In April of that year Mr. E. A. Goldman and I visited the port of San Blas for the

[1] Mr. John Xantus, who spent several years subsequent to 1859 on the west coast of Mexico, was supposed to have visited the islands, on account of several specimens of birds which he sent to the Smithsonian Institution, labeled "Tres Marias Islands, 1861." But as no one else has collected any of these species, and as Xantus sent in no birds which have been taken by others on the islands, it is safe to conclude that he did not visit the Tres Marias.

purpose of outfitting an expedition to the Tres Marias. A letter to the collector of customs at San Blas, kindly furnished me by the Mexican Minister in Washington, the late Don Matias Romero, proved of the greatest service. The collector of customs rendered every assistance in his power, including the loan of a large open boat 25 feet long, and a letter to his deputy which secured us very pleasant quarters in the custom house on Maria Madre. While preparations for the trip were in progress a party from Socorro, N. Mex., consisting of Prof. C. L. Herrick, his son Harry, and Dr. T. S. Maltby arrived at San Blas, also bound for the Tres Marias, and we made the trip together. On the evening of April 28 the boat crept out of the lagoon, and by the aid of a faint land breeze edged slowly off shore. The islands came in sight the next morning, but it was impossible to reach them for several days, owing to calms, head winds, and the lack of a keel to the boat. The stock of water was on the point of exhaustion when Maria Madre was finally reached, three days later, on the afternoon of May 2.

The landing was made at the settlement at the head of a shallow bay on the east side of the island. Our letters secured a cordial welcome from the customs inspector and the agent of the owner of the islands. In a couple of hours the outfit was snugly installed on the broad upper verandas of the custom house, where our headquarters were located. Collections were made near this place, the island traversed both on foot and horseback, and on May 20 a boat trip was made to the north end of the island and across to San Juanito. On May 23 the party returned to the settlement, and two days later proceeded to Maria Magdalena, where camp was made near the beach for four days. On May 29 we crossed to Maria Cleofa, where we remained two days, and then started, May 31, on the return to the mainland. The wind was fair, and a quick trip was made, San Blas being reached on the evening of June 1.

When Colonel Grayson visited the islands, in 1865, he found a settlement on Maria Madre, but the other islands uninhabited. In the spring of 1897 there was a branch custom-house, with three inspectors, at the main settlement on Maria Madre, which had supervision of the shipment of salt and Spanish cedar. The settlement contained about twenty-five families, all of whom, except the customs inspectors, were in the service of the owner of the islands, Señora Gil de Azcona, who lived in the city of Tepic, on the mainland. In May and June the workmen are employed in salt-making at a lagoon near the south point of the island, where there is a small group of houses. The rest of the year they are occupied in cutting cedar and hauling it to the beach for shipment. The available supply of this valuable timber is now approaching exhaustion. Subsequent to Grayson's visit a settlement of woodcutters was made on the northeast side of Maria Magdalena, and a number of houses were built and a field cleared. We found the place deserted, the houses in ruins, and the field overgrown with thorny bushes.

The amount of land suitable for agriculture upon the islands is very limited and forms but a small percentage of the total area. A few cattle are raised on Maria Madre, but the scanty herbage and great scarcity of water during the long dry season limit this industry to the most insignificant proportions. There is a small field near the settlement, where coarse grass is grown for stock. Attempts have been made to grow corn and beans to supply the residents, but the fierce summer storms of wind and rain, called 'chubascos,' which beat the crops to the ground, have rendered these efforts futile. At present all food supplies are brought from the mainland. A number of years ago a house was built and a field cleared and fenced near the north end of the island for the purpose of growing cotton. A warehouse was also built at the main settlement, but after a trial the owner was forced to abandon the industry, the field and house were deserted, and the place is now overgrown with bushes. Subsequently it was proposed to utilize the agaves, which grow abundantly near the north end of the island, for fiber and for distilling from their fleshy bases the alcoholic product known as 'mescal.' Machinery was obtained, but the owner died before the industry was exploited.

In winter the weather is dry and pleasant, and small coasting steamers stop every now and then to take on wood for fuel, and sailing vessels call for Spanish cedar or, in spring, for salt. In May the inhabitants are obliged to lay in a stock of provisions sufficient for several months, as they are practically cut off from communication with the mainland during summer, when the islands are avoided on account of the storms that sweep over them. Many objects drift out from the Gulf of California after storms and are cast up on the shores. In September, 1896, a great tornado of wind and rain swept over northern Sinaloa and the Gulf of California; the coast lowlands were devastated by the flooded rivers, and crops and forests were alike overwhelmed and swept to sea. In May, 1897, the shore of Maria Madre was still strewn with cornstalks, driftwood, and other wreckage that had been stranded after this storm.

Our obligations to the collector of customs at San Blas and his agent on Maria Madre have already been mentioned, and acknowledgments are due also to the owner of the islands, Señora Gil de Azcona, whose letter procured us the use of horses and other courtesies.

PHYSIOGRAPHY.

The Tres Marias are situated between latitude 21° and 22° and longitude 106° and 107° (see frontispiece). Between the islands and the mainland, 20 miles offshore, lies Isabel Island, only about a mile long and 150 feet high. The soundings in the channel between the mainland and the islands gradually deepen to less than 300 fathoms, but just west of the group the sea bottom drops rapidly to more than 1,500 fathoms. The absence of a deep channel shows that they are continental islands, as distinguished from the oceanic Revillagigedo group, farther west.

The Tres Marias group comprises four islands, San Juanito, Maria Madre, Maria Magdalena, and Maria Cleofa, arranged in a northwest and southeast direction. Maria Madre, the largest, measures about 8 by 15 miles, and rises over 2,000 feet above the sea. North of this, and separated from it by a channel 4 miles wide and 5 or 6 fathoms deep, is San Juanito, an islet 3 or 4 miles in diameter and about 100 feet high. Next southeast of Maria Madre is Maria Magdalena, roughly triangular in outline and 7 or 8 miles across, with its central summit rising to an altitude of about 1,500 feet. A shallow channel 8 miles wide separates it from Maria Madre. Southeast of Maria Magdalena lies Maria Cleofa, the last of the group. It is irregularly rounded in outline, about 3 miles across, and its altitude is apparently much less than 1,320 feet, as given on the charts. The channel between the two last-named islands is about 12 miles wide and much deeper than the others.

With the exception of San Juanito, which is nearly flat with a narrow border of low bluffs along the north shore, the islands are mountainous and rise in successive slopes from the shore to the culminating point near the center. The interior of Maria Madre is occupied by a mountainous ridge extending almost the entire length of the island, but descending to a gently sloping area near each end. The eastern side of the island has the longer slope, while the westward or seaward face is much more abrupt, thus corresponding with the formation of the mountains parallel to the coast on the adjacent mainland. Both slopes of the island are scored at intervals with canyons which usually descend in a nearly direct line to the sea. Maria Magdalena and Maria Cleofa are occupied by a central mountainous elevation, from which canyons descend in all directions to the sea. The northeastern points of both these islands are low, flat, sandy areas of limited extent, and the western faces are rocky and precipitous. Permanent fresh water is very scarce on all the islands. There are three little streams on Maria Madre, which sink several miles from the sea during the dry season, and one each on Maria Magdalena and Maria Cleofa.

The relative situation of the islands, with the narrow, shallow channels between them, shows conclusively that at one time they formed a single island at least 45 or 50 miles long, and at a still earlier stage they must have been connected with the mainland. One of the strongest proofs of this former connection is shown by the correspondence between the fauna and flora. The breaking down of the original island into several smaller ones and the evident continuous encroachment of the sea appear to indicate that the subsidence is still in progress. The country back of the coast on the mainland was, within a comparatively recent period, the scene of great volcanic activity, and the Tres Marias bear evidence of having undergone various oscillations in level. On Maria Madre there are great beds of marine deposits, hundreds of feet above sea level, containing quantities of shells and corals of species now living along the shore. Isabel Island, near the mainland, is of volcanic origin and exhibits similar evidence of having once been a much larger island which is now sinking. Apparently it consists mainly of the remains of an old volcano, and a small crater still occupies the center of the island. Although no craters were seen on the Tres Marias, yet there are lavas and other volcanic rocks on all the islands, but a large part of the formation is made up of other rocks elevated by the volcanic uplift.

FAUNA.

The Tres Marias, like the adjacent coast, lie within the Arid Tropical life zone. The evidence furnished by the fauna of the former connection of the Tres Marias with the mainland is as follows: Six species of land shells were obtained, which, according to Dr. William H. Dall, are widely distributed on the mainland. These species are *Polygyra rentrosula* Pfr., *Orthalicus undatus* Brug., *Orthalicus undatus melanocheilus* Val., *Lamellaxis* ——?, *Opeas subula* Pfr., and *Glandina turris*, Pfr. A fresh-water fish taken on Maria Magdalena and Maria Cleofa has been identified by Prof. B. W. Evermann as *Agonostomus nasutus* Günther, a common species on the mainland. In fresh-water pools on Maria Magdalena two or three individuals of another small fish were seen, which were very similiar to common mainland species of *Awaous*, and undoubtedly belong to this or a closely allied genus. Six of the seven species of lizards inhabit the mainland, and only one is peculiar to the islands; the mud turtle and crocodile are also found on the mainland, as are the eight species of snakes. Concerning the reptilian fauna Dr. Stejneger remarks: "Thus most of the species are common on the opposite mainland and generally distributed over tropical Mexico and Central America. Then again it seems as if the species are practically identical on all the islands of the group. This would indicate a comparatively recent severance of these islands from each other, as well as from the opposite mainland of Mexico."

The birds and mammals seem to have been more susceptible to modifying influences than other forms of life. Thirty-six species of resident land birds were found on the group, of which twelve are identical with those on the mainland, and twenty-four can be distinguished specifically or subspecifically. We found ten species of indigenous mammals, seven of which, according to Dr. Merriam, are peculiar to the islands, but closely related to species living on the mainland.

ANIMALS PECULIAR TO THE TRES MARIAS.

So far as known, the following species and subspecies (with the exception of *Compsothlypis insularis*) are peculiar to the islands:

MAMMALS.

Marmosa insularis Merriam.
Oryzomys nelsoni Merriam.
Peromyscus madrensis Merriam.
Lepus graysoni Allen.

Procyon lotor insularis Merriam.
Rhogeëssa parvula H. Allen.
Glossophaga mutica Merriam.

BIRDS.

Columba flavirostris madrensis Nelson.
Leptotila capitalis Nelson.
Buteo borealis fumosus Nelson.
Polyborus cheriway pallidus Nelson.
Psittacula insularis Ridgway.
Trogon ambiguus goldmani Nelson.
Dryobates scalaris graysoni Baird.
Nyctidromus albicollis insularis Nelson.
Amazilia graysoni Lawrence.
Iache lawrencei Ridgway.
Platypsaris aglaiæ insularis (Ridgway).
Myiopagis placens minimus Nelson.
Icterus graysoni Cassin.

Cardinalis cardinalis mariæ Nelson.
Piranga bidentata flammea (Ridgway).
Vireo flavoviridis forreri (Von Madarasz).
Vireo hypochryseus sordidus Nelson.
Compsothlypis insularis (Lawrence). Occurs also on the mainland near San Blas.
Granatellus francescæ Baird.
Thryothorus lawrencii (Ridgway).
Thryothorus lawrencii magdalenæ Nelson.
Melanotis cœrulescens longirostris Nelson.
Myadestes obscurus insularis Stejneger.
Merula graysoni Ridgway.

REPTILES.

Cnemidophorus mariarum Günther.

FLORA.

The islands were visited near the end of the long dry season, when most of the herbaceous plants were withered and lifeless, but representatives of 136 species, largely shrubs and trees, were secured.

The general appearance of the vegetation was the same as that in similar situations on the mainland. Among the most notable plants were the Spanish cedar (*Cedrela*), three species of wild fig (*Ficus*), two of *Pithecolobium*, five of *Solanum*, two of *Ipomœa*, a *Passiflora*, cassias, euphorbias, a large agave, a large cereus, and two opuntias.

On San Juanito the vegetation is largely made up of bushes and scrubby trees 8 to 15 feet high, with many agaves on the sandy southern end. Agaves are very numerous also on the northern end of Maria Madre. On the latter island the forest is rather low and scrubby near the shore, but increases in luxuriance farther up the slopes, especially along the bottoms and sides of the canyons, where Spanish cedars, wild figs, and several other trees attain a large size. In its primeval condition, before the advent of woodcutters, it must have presented a fine example of tropical forest growth. Now, only a few specimens remain to show what the original condition must have been. Along the summit of the island the dense forest is made up of slender-trunked trees, called 'palo prieto' by the natives, which I was unable to identify. On Maria Magdalena the conditions were similar to those on Maria Madre, but a larger percentage of the original forest still remains intact, although the Spanish cedars are mainly gone. Maria Cleofa is more rocky and sterile, and the trees are stunted and brushy. Several species found on the other islands appeared to be wanting here. The report on the plants shows that the flora of the islands is very similar to that of the mainland, and the fact that several new species were found may be due to our imperfect knowledge of the mainland flora.

PLANTS DESCRIBED FROM THE TRES MARIAS.

Ægiphila pacifica Greenman.
Beloperone nelsoni Greenman.
Buxus pubescens Greenman.
Cordia insularis Greenman.
Erythrina lanata Rose sp. nov. (also on mainland).
Euphorbia nelsoni Millspaugh.
Euphorbia subcærulea tresmariæ Millsp. var. nov.

Gilibertia insularis Rose sp. nov.
Pilocarpus insularis Rose sp. nov.
Ternostroemia maltbya Rose sp. nov. (also on mainland).
Zanthoxylum insularis Rose sp. nov.
Zanthoxylum nelsoni Rose sp. nov.

SUMMARY.

The following statement shows the number of species of animals and plants now known from the Tres Marias:

Land mammals	11	Fresh-water shrimp	1
Birds	83	Land mollusks	6
Reptiles	18	Plants	136
Fresh-water fish	2		

ACKNOWLEDGMENTS.

Much of the value of this report is due to the cordial cooperation of several eminent specialists. Through the courtesy of Mr. F. V. Coville, curator of the National Herbarium, Dr. J. N. Rose, assistant curator, was enabled to prepare the report on the plants. Dr. Leonhard Stejneger, curator of the division of reptiles of the National Museum, Dr. William H. Dall, honorary curator of the division of conchology, and Miss Mary J. Rathbun, assistant in the division of invertebrates, reported on the Tres Marias material; and Prof. B. W. Evermann, ichthyologist of the United States Fish Commission, kindly identified the collection of fishes from the islands and the adjacent mainland. Finally, I wish to express my great indebtedness to Mr. Robert Ridgway, curator, and Dr. Charles W. Richmond, assistant curator, of the division of birds in the National Museum, for having so freely placed at my disposal, not only the material in their charge but also their knowledge of tropical American birds.

MAMMALS OF THE TRES MARIAS ISLANDS.

By E. W. Nelson.

Mammals are not numerous either in species or individuals upon the Tres Marias. So far as known, they number but eleven species, of which seven are peculiar to the islands; one is introduced, and the other three are widely ranging bats. A sea lion and two species of porpoise were found near the shores, and whales were reported to occur during certain seasons. As with the birds, one of the most unaccountable features of the mammal fauna is the absence of a number of species that are common on the adjacent mainland. Considering the primitive condition of the islands, it is difficult to explain the presence of field mice, the pigmy opossum, rabbit, and raccoon, while the large gray opossum, nasua, skunk, fox, coyote, deer, peccary, squirrel, and various small rodents of the adjacent mainland remain unrepresented. The Tres Marias mouse was rather common above 200 feet on all of the larger islands; the rabbit was very numerous near the north end of Maria Madre, on San Juanito, and in some places on Maria Magdalena, and two species of bats were abundant in caves on Maria Madre. Aside from these species, mammals were uncommon and difficult to find. One cause of their general scarcity may be the very limited supply of permanent fresh water, and the absence of small species from a broad belt near the shore was easily accounted for by the abundance of carnivorous crabs.

The mammals obtained by our party have been identified by Dr. C. Hart Merriam, who has described the new forms and given critical notes on other species.[1] Of the land mammals taken, five were new and two, *Lepus graysoni* and *Rhogeëssa parvula*, had been previously described. We failed to secure two species of bats (*Myotis nigricans* and *Lasiurus borealis mexicanus*) which were taken by Mr. Forrer. Notwithstanding the fact that collections were made in several branches of natural history, I feel confident that representatives of all the resident land mammals were secured, but it is quite possible that future work may add other bats to the present list.

ANNOTATED LIST OF SPECIES.

Marmosa insularis Merriam. Tres Marias Pigmy Opossum.

   Marmosa insularis Merriam. Proc. Biol. Soc., Washington, XII, pp. 14–15, Jan. 27, 1898. Type from Maria Madre Island.

These pretty little opossums were not found except in the high interior of Maria Madre, between 1,200 and 1,800 feet above sea level, where

---

[1] Proc. Biol. Soc. Washington, XII, pp. 13–19, 1898.

they were apparently rather common about the wild fig trees in the forest and were feeding upon the figs. They may occur also on the other islands, especially upon Maria Magdalena. Two men living on the island described the nests of these animals as globular masses of dry leaves and small plant stems, lined with shreds of softer vegetable matter. The nests are built in the forks of bushes, from 3 to 8 feet from the ground, and have the entrance on the lower side. One of the men found a nest situated as described and about 3 feet from the ground. He saw the owner peering out of a hole near the lower side, but as he approached the head vanished, and the entrance was suddenly closed by the opossum drawing some of the nest material across it. The nest was quickly thrust into a game bag, and when examined was found to contain a female opossum and a number of young clinging to her fur with their feet and tails twined closely about hers. The weight of the young was so great that the parent could only walk very slowly.

Oryzomys nelsoni Merriam.   Nelson's Rice Rat.

    Oryzomys nelsoni Merriam. Proc. Biol. Soc. Washington, XII, p. 15, Jan. 27, 1898. Type from Maria Madre Island.

This rice rat is probably a rare species, as only a few specimens were secured after much trapping. They were found only in damp places near springs about the summit of Maria Madre, about 1,800 feet above sea level. This seemed the most suitable location for them on account of the juicy herbaceous vegetation mingled with the undergrowth.

Peromyscus madrensis Merriam.   Tres Marias Mouse.

    Peromyscus madrensis Merriam. Proc. Biol. Soc. Washington, XII, p. 16, Jan. 27, 1898. Type from Maria Madre Island.

This is the mostly widely distributed and probably the most numerous rodent. Specimens were taken on the three large islands, but its occurrence on San Juanito, where land crabs are very numerous, is doubtful. They were generally distributed over the forest-grown slopes bordering the shore, above the belt infested by crabs. On Maria Madre they were most common about the wild fig trees near the summit (1,500 to 1,800 feet), where the pigmy opossums were secured. Here their burrows entered the ground under logs or projecting roots, but elsewhere these mice were found living beneath rocks and small ledges. They are apparently restricted to the forest, and while nowhere so abundant as were the rabbits in one place near the north end of Maria Madre, yet they were much more generally distributed.

Mus rattus Linn.   Black Rat.

These rats were found in small numbers about the houses and distributed over the forested parts of Maria Madre and, as on the mainland of western Mexico, we found only the gray form.

Lepus graysoni Allen.   Tres Marias Cottontail.

    Lepus graysoni Allen, Mon. N. Am. Rodentia, pp. 347-348, 1877. Type from Tres Marias Islands (undoubtedly from Maria Madre).

The cottontail is abundant in some places on San Juanito, Maria Madre and Maria Magdalena, and was reported to occur on Maria

Cleofa. They were very numerous about a deserted ranch on the north side of Maria Magdalena, but were rather scarce elsewhere on that island. We found them extraordinarily abundant and surprisingly tame about old fields on an abandoned ranch at the northern end of Maria Madre. Some were killed with stones near camp, and it would have been easy to kill over a hundred in a morning. They would sit in their forms among the bushes while one peered at them from a distance of a few feet, and when driven out into an open space they often sat quietly while the camera was brought up and focussed within a short distance. The old fields at this ranch had been long abandoned and were covered with a scattered growth of bushes, which seemed more suitable for the rabbits than the forested areas, where they occurred much more sparingly. The cottontails frequented the wood roads leading from the shore up over the forested slopes, and after 3 o'clock in the afternoon could be found sitting quietly in little open places in the undergrowth waiting for the nearer approach of sunset before coming out into the roads.

The skin of these rabbits was surprisingly delicate, and it was difficult to skin them without tearing it in many places. It was found almost impossible to carry a specimen by the hind legs even a short distance without having the skin tear and slip where it had been grasped by the hand.

It is strange that the rabbits are not more abundant on the islands, considering the fact that the raccoon is the only predatory mammal, and that the few red-tailed hawks and caracaras are the only birds that prey upon them.

Procyon lotor insularis Merriam. Tres Marias Raccoon.

Procyon lotor insularis Merriam. Proc. Biol. Soc. Washington, XII, p. 17, January 27, 1898.

The raccoon was rather common on Maria Madre and Maria Magdalena, but no signs of them were seen on Maria Cleofa, where, however, they may occur. In May they were feeding on wild figs and other fruits and on the crabs, which were very abundant near the shore. Every morning freshly made raccoon tracks were seen in trails leading from the seashore to higher parts of the islands, but the animals usually passed our traps without paying the slightest attention to the bait. They were semi-diurnal in habits and several were seen in the woods in broad daylight. One afternoon one was seen crossing the bed of a dry wash near the northern end of Maria Madre, and instead of trying to escape through the woods it climbed a wild-fig tree on the bank and stood looking down from a horizontal branch until shot.

Zalophus californianus (Lesson). Sea Lion.

A large seal or sea lion, called 'lobo marino' or sea wolf by the Mexicans, was reported to occur at several places on the rocky shores of Maria Magdalena and Maria Cleofa. We first heard of them before leaving San Blas and again upon reaching the islands. It was evident that the sea lions had been hunted for sport by previous visitors until they had become comparatively scarce and are now in a fair way to become extinct. After learning the location of the most frequented places on both islands, we visited them under the guidance of a tortoise-shell hunter who was very familiar with the shore, but we saw only a single sea lion. It was on a rocky islet off the shore of Maria Cleofa, and took to the water and disappeared before we could get a shot. Our guide said that sometimes the sea lions leave the islands for a few days, and this may account for the failure to find them about their usual haunts. The consensus of opinion among the residents of Maria Madre was that these animals are now very scarce. Formerly they were found in many places; but at present a rocky point on the north-west side and a jutting reef on the south side of Maria Magdalena and some islets west of Maria Cleofa are the only landing places used.

It is possible that the Guadalupe Island fur seal (*Arctocephalus townsendi* Merriam) may also occur at times about the islands.

Rhogeëssa parvula H. Allen.   Tres Marias Rhogeëssa.

> *Rhogeëssa parvula* H. Allen.   Proc. Acad. Nat. Sci. Phila., 1866, p. 285.   Type from the Tres Marias.

These little bats were rather common on Maria Madre, where they live in the forest and fly at dusk along the trails and about small open places. At times they appear in such situations in broad day. Two were killed while flying up and down a trail in the brilliant sunshine in the middle of the forenoon, and I saw one hawking for insects among the tree tops along a trail two hours before sunset. As a rule, however, they only come out when it is too dark for one to see more than an indistinct form as they flit about among the trees. A few were also seen on Maria Magdalena.

Myotis nigricans (Maximilian).   Maximilian's Black Bat.

According to Mr. Oldfield Thomas, a specimen of this bat was taken on the Tres Marias by Mr. Forrer.[1] We took none, and they probably occur on the island only as stragglers.

Otopterus mexicanus (Saussure).   Big-eared Bat.

A colony of over a hundred big-eared bats was living in an old ware-house at the settlement on Maria Madre, and others were found in sev-eral caves situated in various parts of the island. The warehouse where these bats were found had a large open window and wide cracks, so that it was quite light inside, yet they were found hanging from the ceiling and roof, in plain view, and evidently had lived there a long time. The specimens were mostly females heavy with young.

Glossophaga mutica Merriam.   Tres Marias Glossophaga.

> *Glossophaga mutica* Merriam.   Proc. Biol. Soc. Washington, XII, pp. 18–19, Jan-uary 27, 1898.   Type from Maria Madre Island.

This was by far the most numerous bat on Maria Madre, where it was found in every cave sufficiently deep to be dark. One cave was among

---

[1] Biologia Centrali-Americana, Mammalia, 206, 1881 (under *Vespertilio nigricans*).

some huge projecting rocks lying at the water's edge, near the settlement. Many of the females collected contained large embryos. These bats were feeding on the fruit of the wild fig.

As surmised by Dr. Merriam,[1] the record of *Charonycteris mexicana* from these islands, given by Mr. Thomas in the Biologia, proves to be referable to the present species. In reply to a letter of inquiry, Mr. Thomas states that he discovered the mistake in identification too late to correct it in the Biologia, and agrees with Dr. Merriam in referring his specimen to *G. mutica.*

Lasiurus borealis mexicanus (Saussure). Mexican Red Bat.

Forrer added this species to the fauna of the Tres Marias as recorded by Mr. Thomas.[2] We did not see any red bats, and I doubt their being found on the islands except as stragglers from the mainland. Bats are such wide ranging animals it is to be expected that several additional species will eventually be found to occur on the islands.

? Phocæna communis (Lesson). Common Porpoise.

Porpoises supposed to belong to this species were common around the shores of the Tres Marias and also in bays and mouths of streams or lagoons along the coast of the mainland. They were always seen in the belt of shallow discolored water within a short distance of the shore. As soon as blue water, with a depth of over 40 fathoms, was reached, the other porpoise (*Prodelphinus longirostris*) was encountered. The common porpoise was seen in schools of 10 to 30 or 40 individuals swimming in loose order. At Maria Madre they came into the shallow bay in front of the settlement in the early morning and followed close along shore.

Prodelphinus longirostris (Gray). Long-nosed Porpoise.

In the blue water between the mainland and the islands these porpoises were very abundant in schools of from 100 to 200 individuals. They are much slenderer and more graceful animals than the preceding species. While swimming about their feeding places at sea they were accompanied by swarms of terns, gannets, and shearwaters. On one occasion, while crossing to the islands, a school of about 200 porpoises came directly toward us and passed under and on all sides of the boat. While they were passing, the water was broken into foam on every hand by their glistening black bodies, and overhead swarmed a shrieking crowd of sea birds. Mr. Goldman made a fortunate rifle shot and killed two of them, but one sank before it could be harpooned.

[1] Proc. Biol. Soc. Washington, XII, pp. 13–19, footnote, January, 1898.
[2] Biologia Centrali-Americana, Mamm., p. 205, footnote.

BIRDS OF THE TRES MARIAS ISLANDS.

By E. W. NELSON.

The present paper is based mainly upon the birds found on the Tres
Marias, but for the sake of completeness the results of our work on
Isabel Island have also been introduced.[1] The situation of Isabel
Island between the mainland and the Tres Marias renders its bird life
of peculiar interest in the present connection. Mr. Xantus sent specimens of birds to the National Museum labeled 'Tres Marias, 1861,'
but only one of these can be an authentic island species, and it seems
almost certain that Xantus did not visit the islands.

Colonel Grayson's notes on his three visits to the group and his
trip to Isabel Island were published by George N. Lawrence in the
'Proceedings' and 'Memoirs of the Boston Society of Natural History,'
while the descriptions of new birds in his collections appeared in various
publications and are mentioned in the bibliography (see pp. 93–94).
Grayson constantly refers to the 'Tres Marias Islands,' but the internal
evidence of his writings, in addition to the information given me by the
inhabitants, indicates that all of his work was done on Maria Madre.

Mr. A. Forrer visited Maria Madre in 1881, but the publication of
Vireo flavoviridis forreri by Von Madarasz and a few notes in the
'Biologia Centrali-Americana' and in some of the British Museum
Catalogues are all we know of his work there.

As already stated in the general introduction, our work was done on
Isabel Island on April 22 and 23, on Maria Madre from May 2 to 25,
and six days were spent working about Maria Magdalena and Maria
Cleofa. It is quite certain that the bird fauna of Maria Madre is
now fairly well known, and it will be advisable for anyone visiting this
group in the future to give attention chiefly to the two smaller islands.
It is certain that a large proportion of the birds found on Maria Madre
occur also on Maria Magdalena, but some of the species living in the
dense forest at higher altitudes on these islands probably do not occur
in the more scanty forest of Maria Cleofa.

At present 83 species and subspecies of birds are known from the
Tres Marias, and further observations will, no doubt, add to the list
various stragglers from the mainland. The bird fauna may be grouped
under the following headings: Resident land birds, 36 species or sub-

[1] The notes in the following pages refer to Isabel Island only when so stated.

21

species. Visitant land birds, 26 species or subspecies. Resident water fowl, 13 species. Visitant water fowl, 8 species.

Of the 36 resident species or subspecies of land birds all but 5 were observed by Colonel Grayson. These exceptions are: *Melopelia leucoptera*, *Tyrannus melancholicus couchi*, *Ornithion imberbe*, *Vireo flaroriridis forreri*, and *Thryothorus lawrencii magdalenœ*.

Twenty-four of the 36 resident land birds are specifically or subspecifically distinct from their mainland representatives. Of this number 12 were described from Grayson's collections, 1 from Forrer's, and 11 from our own. A study of our collections from the islands, and near San Blas on the mainland, brings out the interesting fact that several species from the latter district show a decided approach to their island representatives. This is very marked in *Compsothlypis* which is very nearly the same at San Blas as on the islands. The *Polyborus* and *Platypsaris* from that locality seem to be intermediate between the island races and the birds of the mainland. Specimens of *Thryothorus felix* from the same part of the coast are much nearer *T. lawrencii* than they are to typical *T. felix*.

Among the 24 species or subspecies of land birds peculiar to the islands 15 are larger than their relatives of the nearest mainland. These are *Columba f. madrensis*, *Leptotila capitalis*, *Psittacula insularis*, *Dryobates s. graysoni*, *Nyctidromus a. insularis*, *Amazilia graysoni*, *Icterus graysoni*, *Cardinalis c. mariœ*, *Piranga b. flammea*, *Vireo f. forreri*, *Vireo h. sordidus*, *Compsothlypis insularis*, *Granatellus francescœ*, *Thryothorus lawrencii* and *Merula graysoni*.

Six of the island birds average smaller than their mainland representatives. These are *Polyborus c. pallidus*, *Iache lawrencei*, *Platypsaris a. insularis*, *Myiopagis p. minimus*, *Melanotis c. longirostris*, and *Trogon a. goldmani*. The two first named are generally smaller, but *Platypsaris a. insularis* has a longer tarsus, *Myiopagis p. minimus* a longer bill and tarsus, *Melanotis c. longirostris* a longer bill, and *Trogon a. goldmani* a longer bill and tarsus.

Although *Compsothlypis insularis* also occurs in a limited area along the coast, I have considered it as a typical island species. The difference in size between island birds and their mainland representatives varies greatly, being slight in some and very well marked in others. *Nyctidromus a. insularis* is a larger bird than *albicollis* proper, but has a shorter bill and tarsus. Among the birds peculiar to the islands *Thryothorus lawrencii magdalenœ* and *Myadestes o. insularis* are almost the only ones which do not show more or less well-defined differences in size from their nearest mainland relative; a series of the first named, however, may show that it also differs.

One of the most puzzling features of the fauna of these islands is the absence of various land birds found on the adjacent mainland. Although the physical conditions appear so much like those of the mainland, yet some change must have occurred to upset nature's fine balance and render these isolated areas unsuitable for many species.

The death by starvation of the Louisiana Tanagers on Maria Madre Island (p. 52) is an example of the manner in which the island fauna may be maintained in its present state. As the climatic conditions on the islands and on the mainland are very similar and the vegetation nearly alike, this paucity of species presents one of the curious problems of distribution.

It would be hard to find an equal area of similar country on the mainland, near San Blas, where so few species of land birds could be found. The only reasonable explanation seems to be the scarcity of water and the long, dry season, which combine to reduce the food supply and perhaps render the country unsuited to some species. It was very surprising to find a total absence on the islands of such common and widely spread mainland genera as *Conurus*, *Momotus*, *Piaya*, *Campephilus*, *Melanerpes*, *Myiozetetes*, *Cissolopha*, *Cyanospiza*, *Pipilo*, *Pyrgisoma*, *Saltator*, and others. The absence of *Pipilo* is especially unexpected, for this genus is represented on Socorro Island, which lies very much farther at sea off the same part of the coast.

ANNOTATED LIST OF SPECIES.

† Brachyrhamphus brevirostris (Vigors.) Short-billed Murrelet.

Brachyrhamphus brevirostris was described from San Blas and *B. hypoleucus* from Cape St. Lucas. Colonel Grayson mentions having seen 'guillemots' at Isabel Island (Mem. Boston Soc. Nat. Hist., II, p. 318, 1874) and off the Tres Marias group (Proc. Boston Soc. Nat. Hist., XIV, p. 288, 1871). This led me to anticipate finding at least one of the species there, and it is with some disappointment that I have to record our failure to see either species about the islands, although I watched for them constantly. From this experience I am inclined to think that they breed only along the coast of Lower California, and visit these islands sporadically.

Larus argentatus smithsonianus Coues. American Herring Gull.

A single immature specimen was taken on San Juanito Island May 22, and a few others were seen. These birds were flying back and forth along a strip of beach where a large colony of blue-footed gannets were breeding, and the gulls probably had an eye on the nesting ground for the purpose of capturing any unprotected eggs. They were noted singly a few times along the shores of the Tres Marias and at Isabel Island. No fully adult individuals were seen.

Larus heermanni Cassin. Heermann's Gull.

On April 23 a fine adult bird of this species was shot on the shore of Isabel Island. In company with its mate it had harried a blue-footed gannet into disgorging a number of small fish upon a rock at the edge of the water, and was picking up the spoils by a series of little downward swoops and hoverings. The gannet had shuffled into the water and was making off, with backward glances at its tormentor, when I drew near. These gulls are bold and noisy aggressors when they wish to take advantage of the gannets, and about the breeding places of the latter they feed largely at the public expense. But few of them were seen about the islands—two or three pairs at Isabel and half a dozen pairs about the Tres Marias. A nest, which had been occupied earlier in the season, was seen on the ledge of a rocky islet off the shore of Maria Cleofa May 30, and full grown young of the year were also seen on the rocks.

Sterna maxima Boddaert. Royal Tern.

None were seen at Isabel Island, although they were not uncommon during April along the mainland coast. During May they were seen in small parties about the shores of all the Tres Marias group, where they probably breed in very limited numbers. The only specimen saved was taken May 31 from a flock of six which was coasting along the beach at Maria Cleofa.

Sterna elegans Gambel. Elegant Tern.

Sterna galericulata Lawr., Mem. Boston Soc. Nat. Hist., II, p. 317 (1874).

Colonel Grayson found these terns on Isabel Island, but none were seen by us.

Sterna fuliginosa crissalis (Lawr.). Pacific Sooty Tern.

Haliplana fuliginosa var. *crissalis* Lawr. (ex Baird MS.), Proc. Boston Soc. Nat. Hist., XIV, pp. 285, 301, June, 1871; Mem. Boston Soc. Nat. Hist., II, p. 318, 1874.

These handsome terns are common about Isabel Island where Colonel Grayson found them breeding. My observations from the last of April to the first of June led me to believe that at this season Isabel Island is their central roosting point. During the week we were cruising about Isabel and the Tres Marias islands many flocks were seen. From about noon until the middle of the afternoon or later the flocks were generally flying directly toward Isabel at an altitude of from 50 to 200 yards above the water. This was noted also near the islands, while we were crossing the straits between the Tres Marias, and off the mainland near San Blas. Many of the birds were perched along the top of an inaccessible rock just off Isabel, and were also seen alighting on the cliffs of the northern and northeastern side of the island, but the boat was too unwieldy for us to venture near enough to closely examine these haunts. The birds have a peculiar shrill cry which they often utter while feeding and when flying about at night. The night before we landed on Isabel Island it was necessary to anchor about midway between the island and the shore. The wind blew strongly in the afternoon but fell at sunset, a dead calm ensued, and heavy clouds overspread the sky. During the day only a few sooty terns had been seen, but from about 9 p. m. until near daybreak they were evidently much more numerous, for their cries were heard at short intervals. Several times the notes were uttered directly overhead and the birds seemed to be scarcely higher than the top of the mast, where they apparently paused and hovered while they examined the boat with great curiosity. As they were heard every night while we were at sea, it is evident that they were both diurnal and nocturnal in habits.

They feed well out at sea, and were not found anywhere along shore, except when they came to their roosting place on Isabel Island. There were no signs of their roosting about the Tres Marias, although they may roost on some of the outlying rocky islets. Grayson found them in small numbers farther west, about the Revillagigedo Islands. During our trip to the Tres Marias many schools of large fish were encountered swimming close to the surface and constantly breaking, often with such force and rapidity that the water boiled and foamed over considerable areas. These schools of fish were commonly accom-panied by flocks of sooty terns and gannets, which appeared to be animated by the wildest excitement. The terns hovered over the foaming sea, uttering shrill cries and darting down into the water, evi-dently after food; and in the midst of the turmoil the blue-footed gan-nets swam about, beating the water with their wings and adding to the noise made by the terns and leaping fish. While on Maria Madre I saw a flock of terns some distance off shore, and taking a canoe, managed to get out to them, and directly in the course of the school of fish they were accompanying. Letting the boat drift, I stood up and watched the swarm go by. Thousands of large fish and hundreds of terns and gannets passed the boat on every side, amid loud cries from the terns, a rushing sound from the fish and gannets, and a bewildering complexity of motion in sea and air that was intensely exciting. This novel sight was so interesting that I came near losing the chance to secure some of the birds.

These terns were seen also following schools of porpoises off shore—in the latter case accompanied by the wedge-tailed shearwater. In the passage between Maria Magdalena and Maria Cleofa a flock of sooty terns was seen soaring in wide circles high overhead and finally start-ing off for their roosting place on Isabel Island.

The 'variety *crissalis*,' named in manuscript by Professor Baird and published by Mr. Lawrence, was characterized as "having the under tail coverts tinged with ashy, instead of being pure white." A series of 17 specimens from the west coast of Mexico, and from widely scat-tered islands of the Pacific and Indian oceans, agree in having the posterior part of flanks, under wing coverts, and entire crissum dis-tinctly ashy, not a single individual being white on these parts, as is commonly the case with birds from the Atlantic and Gulf coasts of North America. Unfortunately the series of Atlantic birds at hand is very small, but there is little doubt that *crissalis* is a valid subspe-cies. Birds from the west coast of Mexico, the Galapagos Islands, and Hawaii agree in having an average shorter bill and tail than those from elsewhere. Specimens from the Indian Ocean have even a longer bill and tail than those from the Atlantic, but are ashy below,

like those from western Mexico. Specimens from Ascension Island, off
the west coast of Africa, also have a light ashy shade on the lower
tail coverts.

The following average measurements show the sizes of these birds
from various parts of their range:

Table of measurements of Sterna fuliginosus and Sterna f. crissalis.*

Name.	Locality.	Number of specimens.	Wing.	Tail.	Culmen.	Tarsus.
Sterna fuliginosus ..	East coast of North America and west coast of Africa.	7	208.1	151	42.8	23.5
Sterna fuliginosus crissalis.	West coast of Mexico, Hawaii, and Galapagos Islands.	10	288.6	143.5	41.8	23.6
Sterna fuliginosus crissalis.	Krusenstern Islands (west of Hawaii).	2	292.5	203.5	39.5	24.2
Sterna fuliginosus crissalis.	Glorioso Island (Indian Ocean)	3	292.6	192	43.3	23.8

* All measurements are in millimeters.

In the foregoing measurements the length of the tail is unreliable,
owing to its variability, on account of wear and other causes.

Anous stolidus ridgwayi Anthony. Pacific Noddy Tern.

Anous stolidus Lawr., Mem. Boston Soc. Nat. Hist., II, p. 318, 1874.
Anous stolidus ridgwayi Anthony, Auk, XII, p. 36, 1898.

Common the last of April on Isabel Island, and a few seen off the
Tres Marias during May. Between San Blas and the islands a
number of these birds were seen. We usually saw one or two individuals at a time, and did not find them in flocks anywhere except
when congregated on the rocks at their roosting places. At sea they
usually flew close along the surface of the waves with long, graceful
wing strokes. From their dark color and habit of keeping close to the
water they were several times mistaken for black petrels.

They were found in considerable numbers on the ragged faces of
cliffs and rocks along the northeastern point of Isabel Island, and were
very unsuspicious, permitting us to approach quite near in the boat.
While perched on the black lava cliffs, their dark color blended so
closely with the background that it was very difficult to distinguish
them, even when within fair gunshot. The day we left the island we
visited their resting place and fired a dozen or more shots while they
were on the rocks or flying about, but the noise of the reports did not
seem to give them much alarm. They would circle out a short distance, and, after hovering for a few moments over their killed or
wounded companions floating in the water, would return to the same
part of the cliff from which they had just been startled. They were
not heard to utter any notes, and the silence with which they would
suddenly appear out of the cliff and then return and vanish again in
its gloomy face produced an uncanny effect.

Colonel Grayson found them nesting on the north end of Isabel Island in April, 1869, and states that they were breeding in communities on shelving rocks beneath overhanging cliffs. The nests were placed close together, but were inaccessible. A single egg was procured, however, which was white, with scattering brownish blotches, most numerous about the larger end. This is undoubtedly the tern which Colonel Grayson reports as replacing the sooty tern on the Revillagigedo Islands, and which be described as being black, with a hoary forehead.

Puffinus cuneatus Salvin. Wedge-tailed Shearwater.

Puffinus cuneatus Salvin, Ibis, 5th ser., VI, p. 353, July, 1888.
Puffinus knudseni Stejn., Proc. U. S. Nat. Mus., XI, p. 93, Nov. 8, 1888.

During our trip to and from the islands we saw 100 or 200 wedge-tailed shearwaters. They were usually seen singly skimming along over the sea, at an elevation of a few yards, making widely sweeping circuits and pausing occasionally to pick up bits of food. When about midway between Isabel Island and the Tres Marias we encountered several schools of small porpoises of 150 or more individuals, which traveled in close array, frequently gamboling about and playfully leaping high in the air. A swarm of sooty terns followed the porpoises, and twice when they passed near us I saw considerable numbers of these shearwaters among the terns. Judging from the numbers, they must be rather common in these waters, but none were seen near the islands.

This species was first described from specimens taken on the Krusenstern Islands, in the Marshall Group, and Mr. A. W. Anthony made the first record of its occurrence on the American side of the Pacific, at the Revillagigedo Islands, during the summer of 1897 (Auk, XV, Jan., 1898, p. 39). As it is a species new to North America, a detailed description of our specimen is given, in order to facilitate identification in case other examples should be taken.

Description.—No. 156678, U. S. Nat. Mus., Dept. of Agriculture Coll. Ad. ♂, off Maria Madre Island, May 2, 1897. Collected by E. W. Nelson and E. A. Goldman.

Top and sides of head and neck grayish-brown; forehead, lores, and space from latter area back beneath eyes and along sides of neck paler or more ashy, thus edging the darker area of the crown and upper neck with lighter. Back, including rump and upper tail coverts, mainly dark brown, but mixed with numerous feathers of a decidedly grayish, almost ashy, shade. These latter feathers undoubtedly indicate the color of dorsal surface in fresh-plumaged birds. Wings and tail blackish-brown. Entire lower surface of body white, shaded with dingy ashy, darkest on sides and palest along median portion. Under tail coverts mixed dark brown and grayish-brown. Border of the wing along under side brown or grayish-brown; under coverts white with a little flecking of pale gray on some feathers. In the flesh this specimen had a horn-blue bill with flesh-colored feet and tarsi.

Dimensions.—Wing, 293; tail, 135 (length of middle pair of tail feathers beyond lateral pair, 47); culmen, 42; tarsus, 50; middle toe, with claw, 59.

Habitat.—The range of this species is now known to extend across the middle North Pacific from Japan to the west coast of Mexico.

Oceanodroma melania (Bonap.).   Black Petrel.

Common between Isabel and the Tres Marias. Black petrels were by far the most numerous of the petrels seen, and outnumbered all the others two to one. Three, and possibly four, other species were seen on the way to and from the islands, but this was the only one secured. They circled about in all directions, sometimes coming very near, but nothing peculiar in their habits was observed. They were quick to see little fragments of fat thrown overboard while we were skinning other waterfowl, and when the morsels were small enough ate them greedily.

Phæthon æthereus Linn.   Red-billed Tropic Bird.

Tropic birds are readily distinguished on the wing by their graceful ternlike flight and long filamentous tail feathers. Many of them breed on Isabel Island and in suitable places on rocky islets near San Blas and about the Tres Marias. The last of April fresh eggs and nearly grown young were found on Isabel, and by the last of May the young on the Tres Marias had taken wing and few were to be seen, although we were told by the tortoise shell hunters that many breed there earlier in the season.

Soon after landing on Isabel, a tropic bird was found sitting on its solitary egg at the end of a little hole in the rock close to the beach. The hole was only about 15 or 18 inches across and about 3 feet deep, so that there was no difficulty in taking the bird by hand after a little maneuvering to avoid its sharp beak. During a stay of about twenty-four hours on this island at least 20 nests containing eggs or young were examined. A single egg is laid directly on the rough rock or loose dirt forming the floor of the nesting site, which is always located under the shelter of over arching rock, but varies greatly in situation. The inner ends of holes in cliffs facing the sea were favorite places, but as the number of such situations was limited, the birds were forced to utilize small caves and even rock shelters. In one locality five or six nests were placed on loose earth at the bottom of rock shelters so situated that I could walk directly up to them and pick up the birds. Whenever a nest was approached the parent screamed and fought viciously, ruffled its feathers and looked very fierce, but made no attempt to escape. They protested with beak and voice when pushed about, but as soon as I went away a few yards they would shuffle back to resume their former position over the egg. The young, even when quite small, were equally fierce in resenting any intrusion. One nest was found on the beach under the edge of some great rocks that had fallen from the adjacent cliff. It was only 5 or 6 feet above high tide and would have been overlooked but for the angry cries of the old bird when she heard me walking over the roof of her habitation. At sunrise the old birds were found sitting side by side at the mouths of their nesting places waiting to enjoy the first rays of sunlight. Half an hour later one of each pair started out to sea while the other resumed its place on the nest. When disturbed on the nest their cries are very shrill and strident, consisting of a series of short, harsh, clicking or rattling sounds something like the noise of an old-fashioned watchman's rattle. The young are covered at first with fluffy white down. Before they are one-third grown the first plumage begins to appear, and is very similar to that of the adults, except that the black barring on the back is broader.

Sula websteri Rothschild.   Webster's Booby.

Sula bassana Grayson, Proc. Boston Soc. Nat. Hist., p. 302, 1871.
Sula websteri Rothschild, Bull. Brit. Orn. Club, VII, No. LIV, p. LII, 1898.

This booby is no doubt the *Sula bassana* reported from Isabel Island by Grayson but not seen by us. Mr. Anthony found it the most abundant species breeding on the Revillagigedo Islands during the summer of 1898.

Sula brewsteri Goss.   Brewster's Booby.

Sula brewsteri Goss, Auk V, p. 242, 1888.

Brewster's boobies were very numerous on a small hill at one side of the little bay where we landed on Isabel Island April 22, but there were no signs of their breeding. They came in from sea during the first half of the afternoon and sat about on rocky parts of the shore until nightfall. Scattered individuals were also seen about the ledges and tops of the cliffs facing the sea. The following morning at daybreak they were congregated on the little hill already mentioned which is probably their regular roosting place. About half an hour after sunrise they began to start out to sea singly and by twos and threes until all were off on the day's fishing expedition. A few were seen about the rocks just off San Blas, and were said to breed on the large rock (Piedra Blanca) midway between Isabel and San Blas. Only a few of these boobies were seen about the Tres Marias until an islet was visited off the northwest shore of Maria Cleofa. This islet rises from 150 to 200 feet above the sea, with cliffs on all sides. The summit is mainly rolling, with an elevated, sloping bench on one end   At this time, May 30, many thousands of boobies were breeding on the bare top of this rock. The eggs were laid directly on the surface, with no sign of a nest. The sun was intensely hot and heated the rocks so that they were uncomfortably warm to the touch. The birds did not sit upon the eggs during the hottest hours, but while standing to avoid contact with the heated rocks kept in such position that the eggs or young were shaded from the sun, and thus had their vitality preserved. While trying to secure photographs of this breeding ground a few of the old birds flew away and it was surprising to see how quickly the newly hatched young succumbed to the heat when the parents left them exposed to the rays of the sun. The nests were spaced at intervals of 4 or 5 feet, so that the old birds were safely out of reach of one another. Although so gregarious in their breeding habits, they appeared to have but little regard for one another. It was amusing to see the savage way in which the nest owners assisted intruders of their own kind out of their territory. While we were walking among them some of the birds would often waddle off to one side, and in so doing necessarily trespassed on their neighbors. The latter at once raised a hoarse shrieking and set upon the outsiders with wicked thrusts of their beaks, which continued until the victims took wing and escaped. We were also subjects of this proprietary rage, and had our legs nipped every now and then, despite all efforts to walk circumspectly. Our progress over the breeding ground was accompanied by a wave of hoarse, nasal cries that sometimes became almost deafening. Many of the birds were valiant upholders of their rights and sturdily refused to leave their nests, which they defended vigorously, all the time uttering loud cries of rage.

These birds show very little individual variation in color. As the species is not well known the following descriptions are appended from specimens taken on Isabel and Maria Cleofa.

Adult male.—Nearly entire head white, shading gradually on posterior portion into drab of neck and then insensibly into dark, sooty brown of back. On lower side of neck the drab becomes darkest at posterior border, where it ends abruptly against the pure white of lower parts. Bill light horn color; gular pouch in life livid blue; feet greenish yellow—the latter varying in intensity.

Male in immature plumage.—Dorsal surface uniform dark brown, slightly paler than back of adult; entire lower surface still paler and more dingy brown. Feathers over much of body, especially about head, neck, and lower parts, narrowly edged with grayish brown, giving a faint wavy barring. Bill bluish horn color, with darker shade of same about base and on gular pouch; feet and tarsi dull fleshy yellow; iris greenish gray.

Adult female.—Head, neck all around, and back sooty brown; ventral surface below neck white. Bill light horn color; a spot of leaden bluish on lores; base of bill, gular pouch, feet, and tarsi grayish yellow; iris pale grayish.

Average measurements of these birds from Isabel Island are as follows: ♂ (5 specimens), wing 384.4; tail 189.6; culmen 93.6; tarsus 45.4; ♀ (5 specimens), wing 416.6; tail 192.8; culmen 96.6; tarsus 48.8.

Nestlings a few days old are covered with fluffy white down. A male bird of the previous year, which still retained the immature plumage, was taken at Isabel on April 23, and several others were seen.

Sula nebouxii Milne-Edwards. Blue-footed Booby.

Sula piscator Grayson, Proc. Boston Soc. Nat. Hist., XIV, p. 302, 1871; Lawr.,
Mem. Boston Soc. Nat. Hist., II, p. 316, 1874.

Sula nebouxii Milne-Edwards, Ann. Sci. Nat., Paris (Zool.), 6eme sér., XIII, Art.
4, p. 37, pl. 14, 1882 (Chile).

Sula gossi Goss (ex Ridgway MS.), Auk, V, p. 241, July, 1888 (Gulf of Calif.).

Sula nebouxii is the most abundant species of booby occurring on
Isabel and the Tres Marias. On April 22 they were breeding abundantly on the beaches and on a low flat area that covers a part of the
former island. They were common on the grassy beach at the landing
and thence back among the scrubby trees and bushes which form a
scanty growth over the flat. They were most numerous on the open
beach a little above high-water mark, but dozens of them were seen
with their eggs farther back among the bushes. Like the preceding
species, they fought and screamed savagely when approached. The
males usually flew away, but the females remained to give battle over
the nests, which were mere hollows in the earth, sand, or gravel. Not
a single young one was seen in the hundreds of nests on Isabel.

The sun was excessively hot the morning of our arrival, and while
the men were landing the outfit, ropes were fastened between the tops
of some scrubby trees close to the beach and a piece of canvas spread
for an awning, under which the baggage was placed. An old booby
had her eggs in the sand within 3 feet of the edge of the sheltered area
and stood her ground unflinchingly while the men were at work,
keeping a wary eye on their movements and making vicious dabs
whenever a leg came incautiously within reach. Having arranged
camp, I went out exploring for an hour or so and returned with various
specimens, including the egg of a tropic bird, and found that one of the
boatmen had driven off the booby and thrown away her eggs. Wish-
ing to test the bird's discrimination, I placed the reddish-brown egg of
the tropic bird in the hollow where the two greenish-white eggs of the
booby had been, and sitting under the awning began to prepare
specimens. In the course of half an hour the owner of the despoiled
nest returned and alighted 10 or 15 steps away near another deserted
nest, gave a look at the eggs in it, walked to still another, looked at it,
and then proceeded directly to her own nest and stopped. She looked
about and then down at the nest. The presence of the single
reddish-colored egg appeared to surprise her; she looked at it with
one eye and then with the other as if in doubt. An instant later the
feathers on her head and nape ruffled up and with a loud squawk of
rage she suddenly dashed her beak again and again into the strange
egg, breaking it to fragments in a moment. As soon as the egg was
demolished she took wing and disappeared out to sea. There was no
intention to sacrifice the tropic bird's egg in this experiment, so the
booby carried off the honors.

About 10 o'clock the following night a visit was paid to the nesting
boobies. The night was calm, and taking a lighted candle I walked

out a short distance to an opening in the bushes where there were twenty or thirty nests. The females were found on their eggs with the males standing close beside them. When the strange visitor appeared in their midst the birds set up a continuous series of hoarse cries and, like so many moths, seemed to become fascinated by the light. They started up on all sides, and trooping within the circle of bright light, began to run around me in a ring about 20 feet in diameter. They ran in single file from right to left and presented a most ludicrous sight. Occasionally one fell on its breast, whereupon the others scrambled over the fallen bird until it regained its feet and rejoined the procession. One of the number was suddenly possessed with a desire to run around one of my legs, and, although seized by the head several times and tossed out among its companions, persisted in returning to the same place and continuing its gyrations. The next morning at daybreak the birds were seen standing in pairs by their eggs and remained in this position until about sunrise, or a little after, when all of the males went out to sea—usually in little parties of two to five or six. They returned between 1 and 3 o'clock in the afternoon, and a number of them flew directly to their mates and disgorged numerous small fishes which the females ate greedily. These observations seemed to show that the females did the incubating and the males provided the food. As the neighboring waters do not abound in small fishes, the boobies have to go in many cases from 10 to 30 miles to obtain their daily supply. During a visit to San Juanito Island, the latter part of May, many blue-footed boobies were found breeding on sandy beaches at the south end of the island; many of the young were hatched and some were more than half grown. Like the young of the tropic birds, the young boobies uttered angry cries and fought savagely when approached.

This species is found in Chile, on the Galapagos Islands, and north to the island of San Pedro Martir in the Gulf of California. The type of *Sula nebouxii* was obtained on the coast of Chile, and the type of *S. gossi* came from San Pedro Martir.

The sexes are alike in color, but when standing together the males may be readily distinguished by their smaller size and slenderer form. In life the bill is leaden horn color, with its base and the gular pouch leaden blue; the feet are bright blue. The downy young are pure white. Four specimens measure as follows: ♂ (1 specimen), wing, 410; tail, 219; culmen, 108; tarsus, 51. ♀ (average of 3 specimens), wing, 438; tail, 219; culmen, 109.6; tarsus, 56.

Phalacrocorax sp. Cormorant.

Two or three cormorants seen at a distance were the only ones noted during the trip. None were seen near Isabel nor on the rocks near San Blas.

Pelecanus californicus Ridgway. California Brown Pelican.

A few pairs of brown pelicans were breeding on Isabel Island the last of April. The nests were made of sticks and placed in the dense tops of the scrubby trees growing on the rocky inner slopes of the island. They were found about all of the Tres Marias, but usually occurred singly and were nowhere common. Two or three were seen fishing in the breakers alongshore at the north end of Maria Madre.

Fregata aquila (Linn.). Man-o'-war Bird.

Hundreds of man-o'-war birds were breeding on Isabel in April, and on approaching the island many were seen soaring over the rocky summit. The first shot caused hundreds of others to take wing, and in a few moments the air was swarming with them. They soared in constantly intersecting circles, until the sky seemed covered with their silhouetted outlines. So few had been seen alongshore near San Blas that it was an interesting and unexpected sight. Upon landing, numerous large, oval, and brilliantly red objects were seen in the tops of the dark-green bushes along the slopes. These proved to be the gular pouches of old male man-o'-war birds inflated to the size of a man's head, the brilliant red color of the distended membrane making them very conspicuous objects. It appeared to be a common custom of the birds to sit quietly on the top of a tree for a long time with the pouches thus distended and evidently serving as sexual ornaments. A few birds were seen circling high overhead with their pouches fully inflated, but as a general rule, when soaring, the pouches were closed.

The nests were built of sticks and placed in the tops of low trees and stout bushes from near sea level to the summit of the island. Three or four of these platform-like structures were found together in some of the larger bushes. Many of the young were hatched and, when able to stand alone, would do their best with voice and beak to resent our approach. The young are covered with white down until nearly half grown.

A few of these birds were also seen about the Tres Marias, and are said to breed on San Juanito, but were not common.

Ardea herodias Linn. Great Blue Heron.

A few solitary individuals were seen at various times during May along the beaches, and it is probable that a few pairs may breed on the islands. They were also noted by Colonel Grayson.

Ardea egretta Gmel. American Egret.

The American egret is another species noted by Colonel Grayson, which we did not see. It must occur merely as a straggler from the mainland.

Ardea candidissima Gmel. Snowy Heron.

Recorded by Colonel Grayson as a straggler, but not seen by us.

Nycticorax violaceus (Linn). Yellow-crowned Night Heron.

A dozen or more night herons were noted and a young bird was shot on a rock close to Isabel Island, where it must have strayed from the mainland. As Colonel Grayson found them on the islands and took specimens in immature plumage, it is very probable that they breed there in small numbers.

Totanus flavipes (Gmel.). Yellow-legs.

A single specimen was shot by Prof. C. L. Herrick on Maria Madre the middle of May.

Actitis macularia (Linn.). Spotted Sandpiper.

A few were seen along the shore on all of the islands, where they probably breed.

Several small flocks of another sandpiper were seen along shore on the islands; but although considerable energy was expended in their pursuit we failed to secure a specimen.

Ægialitis semipalmata Bonap. Semipalmated Plover.

Colonel Grayson took a single specimen of this plover. It was not seen by us and must occur only as a straggler.

Hæmatopus palliatus Temminck. American Oyster-catcher.

Rather common on the shores of the Tres Marias and Isabel, as well as along the coast of the mainland near San Blas. A series of ten oyster-catchers were secured and have been compared with four specimens of *Hæmatopus galapagensis*, one of *H. frazari*, and a number of typical *H. palliatus* (from the Atlantic coast of the United States and the West Indies).

All of the birds from the Tres Marias, Isabel Island, and the adjacent mainland were found to be surprisingly close to typical *palliatus*. As the Tres Marias are not far south of Lower California, the birds from the islands might naturally be expected to be nearly typical representatives of *H. frazari*. In reality about the only sign of gradation toward the latter form is the mixed black and white across the lower border of the black neck area. Some specimens from a single small flock on Maria Cleofa had the line of demarkation between the black and white areas on the breast as sharply defined as in *palliatus*, while others had the mixed black and white areas, as in *frazari* and *galapagensis*. Some of the birds have a white spot on the under eyelid, which is absent in others, but otherwise the color is the same as in typical *palliatus*. Birds from the Tres Marias and the mainland coast to the south have an average shorter bill and tarsus than true *palliatus*, and in this character approximate *frazari* and *galapagensis*. Mr. Ridgway has already called attention to the close general similarity existing between the two latter species. The series from the Tres Marias and adjacent coast agree with specimens in the National Museum from various points along the Pacific coast of Mexico, Central, and South America in being very close to typical *palliatus*, thus showing pretty conclusively that this is the resident bird along the coast and adjacent islands south of Lower California.

So far as can be judged from specimens at hand, *H. galapagensis* is distinct from *frazari*, although the birds resemble one other more closely than they do representatives of *palliatus* from the adjacent mainland. A series of specimens from the southern end of Lower California will probably show intergradation between *palliatus* and *frazari*. The following measurements show the comparative sizes of birds from various localities:

Measurements of Hæmatopus palliatus, H. frazari, and H. galapagensis.

Name.	Locality.	Sex.	Number of specimens.	Wing.	Tail.	Culmen.	Tarsus.
Hæmatopus palliatus..	Atlantic coast, United States and West Indies.	♀	3	260	102.3	90	63
Hæmatopus palliatus..	Tres Marias and Isabel Islands.	♂	6	256	100.1	75.8	58.1
Hæmatopus palliatus..	Tres Marias and adjacent coast.	♂	5	262.2	104	83.8	58.4
Hæmatopus palliatus..	Peru and Chile..............	♂	2	263	97.5	84	61
Hæmatopus frazari....	Coast of Lower California ..	♂	4	250.2	116.8	74.4	56.9
Hæmatopus galapagensis.	Galapagos Islands	♂	2	253	98	84.5	54.5
Hæmatopus galapagensis.	Galapagos Islands	♂	3	246.6	101.6	82	57

Columba flavirostris madrensis Nelson. Tres Marias Pigeon.

Columba flavirostris Grayson, Proc. Boston Soc. Nat. Hist., XIV, p. 274, 1871; Lawr., Mem. Boston Soc. Nat. Hist., II, p. 301, 1874.

Columba flavirostris madrensis Nelson, Proc. Biol. Soc. Washington, XII, p. 6, 1898.

These handsome birds were rather common on Maria Madre and Maria Magdalena, ranging to the summits of the islands, and they probably live also on Maria Cleofa. On Maria Madre they were most numerous along the wooded sides of a canyon some distance back from the coast, where they usually perched among the higher branches of the trees or were seen flying about by twos and threes. Early in the morning a few could be found among the smaller trees on the bases of the foothills near the settlement, but later in the day they retired farther inland to the more heavily wooded slopes. On Maria Magdalena they were numerous in some trees near a group of deserted houses and in old clearings a short distance back from the shore. They came to these trees to feed upon the ripening fruit, but were rather shy. When one becomes startled and takes wing it makes a loud flapping noise that alarms its companions, and then all dash swiftly away. They were less confiding than most of the birds on the islands, but were not so shy as their representatives on the mainland. Wild figs and the small fruit of a tree, probably a species of *Psidium*, or wild guava, were favorite articles of food. Their loud cooing note is uttered at short intervals and is one of the characteristic sounds in the forests they frequent. They are essentially arboreal in habits and are rarely seen near the ground.

Zenaidura macroura (Linn). Mourning Dove.

A single mourning dove was taken on May 5, on Maria Madre, and a few others were seen on the island during the first half of the month. They were found for a short time about an old field near the shore, and, like several other species, were probably stray migrants.

Leptotila fulviventris brachyptera (Salvadori). White-fronted Dove.

There is a typical specimen of this bird in the National Museum collection, which was taken on the Tres Marias by Colonel Grayson. It was undoubtedly a straggler from the mainland, as it shows no approach toward the characters distinguishing the resident insular species.

Leptotila capitalis Nelson. Tres Marias Dove.

> *Leptoptila albifrons* Grayson, Proc. Boston Soc. Nat. Hist., XIV, p. 274, 1871 (part);
> Lawr., Mem. Boston Soc. Nat. Hist., II, p. 305, 1874 (part).
> *Leptotila capitalis* Nelson, Proc. Biol. Soc. Washington, XII, p. 6, 1898.

Very common on Maria Madre and Maria Magdalena, and probably occurs also on Maria Cleofa. They run about on the ground under the shade of the forest with motions like those of a quail. During the morning and evening hours quiet trails leading through the forest are their favorite resorts. When walking along these trails one sees them for a moment, sometimes running and sometimes on the wing close to the ground, as they disappear around the next bend. If one is walking slowly the birds will frequently keep ahead for some distance, but if pressed they either run or fly to one side into the sheltering woods. They have a loud cooing note, which is heard at short intervals wherever the birds are common. During the hot hours of the day they retire to the shadiest recesses of the forest and usually perch in some thick-topped tree. While resting in these retreats they have the pretty custom of uttering mellow call notes, as if in response to one another. During the breeding season they are seen in pairs, keeping close together, but at other times are solitary. When forced to take wing, they do so with a loud whirring sound and dart away through the intricate mazes of the dense forest with wonderful quickness. Their agility in flying at full speed among the network of trunks and branches is extraordinary and equalled by few birds. If they take wing without being alarmed, their flight is almost noiseless.

Melopelia leucoptera (Linn). White-winged Dove.

White-winged doves were rather common residents on both Maria Madre and Maria Magdalena, and a few were seen on Maria Cleofa.

Colonel Grayson does not mention having seen this bird during any of his visits to the islands. It seems quite improbable that so conspicuous a species should have been present and overlooked, and I am inclined to believe that it has become a resident of the islands since his visits. It is now a conspicuous and widely spread species and one of the two resident land birds found by us that are not in Grayson's list. In habits and appearance the white-winged doves of the islands are identical with those on the mainland, where the species is very numerous. Two specimens were taken on Maria Madre, May 7, and a single specimen was shot on Isabel Island, April 22; the latter was undoubtedly a straggler from the mainland, since Isabel is a waterless island.

Columbigallina passerina pallescens (Baird). Mexican Ground Dove.

These pretty little doves were common on Maria Madre and Maria Magdalena, but were most numerous about old fields and in the settlement on the former island. The series of specimens taken on Maria Madre appears to be identical with the birds of the adjacent mainland; seven males from the islands average as follows: Wing, 87.4; tail, 61.8; culmen, 11.6; tarsus, 16.6.

Cathartes aura (Linn.). Turkey Vulture.

Generally distributed, and very common about the settlement on Maria Madre.

Buteo borealis fumosus Nelson. Tres Marias Red-tailed Hawk.

> *Buteo borealis* var. *montana* Grayson, Proc. Boston Soc. Nat. Hist., XIV, p. 268, 1871 (part).
> *Buteo borealis* var. *calurus* Lawr., Mem. Boston Soc. Nat. Hist., II, p. 301, 1871 (part).
> *Buteo borealis fumosus* Nelson, Proc. Biol. Soc. Washington, XII, p. 7, 1898.

Colonel Grayson records this as a common species. We found a few living along the canyons that score the slopes of Maria Madre. They were very sparsely distributed and only some twelve or fifteen individuals were noted; two or three were seen on Maria Magdalena and none on Maria Cleofa. They were not at all shy, and whenever found perched on a tree were readily approached within gunshot. They feed mainly upon iguanas and rabbits, both of which are common on the two larger islands. Nothing distinctive was noted about the habits of these hawks. They are uniform in color, and differ more from the mainland forms than does *B. borealis socorroensis*, although the latter is from an island much farther out at sea.

The adult female of *fumosus* has some heavy shaft streaks of dark brown on the chest, but these are not heavy enough to form a well-defined dark area as is often the case in *calurus*.

Description of an immature male (?) from Maria Madre: Upper surface almost uniform blackish brown; tail mainly of same color, but crossed by nine narrow, irregular lighter bands; a light area on the throat, where the feathers have narrow blackish shaft lines and broad, dull white borders; breast and sides of neck dull, dark brown, with dull, rusty edgings to feathers on latter area; middle of breast paler; feathers on lower breast and flanks blackish brown, with irregular whitish spots; abdomen and lower tail coverts dull brownish, paler than flanks, with pale buffy barring; some feathers of tibia buffy or heavily barred with buffy, but mostly like those of lower breast.

Below are averages showing the relative size of the two island forms:

Measurements of Buteo borealis fumosus and Buteo b. socorroensis.

Name.	Locality.	Sex	Number of specimens.	Wing.	Tail.	Culmen.	Depth of bill.	Tarsus.
Buteo borealis fumosus.	Maria Madre Island.	Ad. ♂	3	373.3	207.3	26	18.5	81.3
Buteo borealis fumosus.	.... do	Ad. ♀	1	412	214	30	20	84
Buteo borealis socorroensis.	Socorro Island......	Ad. ♂	2	387.5	207.5	25	17.5	80
Buteo borealis socorroensis.	.....do	Ad. ♀	1	425	221	30	20	86

Falco peregrinus anatum (Bonap.). Duck Hawk.

> *Falco peregrinus* var. *nigriceps* Grayson, Proc. Boston Soc. Nat. Hist., XIV, p. 268, 1871.

A single duck hawk was taken by Colonel Grayson, who mentions that it was shot while in close pursuit of a sparrow hawk. We did not see this species during our visit to the islands.

Falco sparverius Linn. Sparrow Hawk.

The sparrow hawk was recorded from the islands by Colonel Grayson, but we did not see a single individual, and it probably occurs merely as a straggler.

Falco columbarius Linn. Pigeon Hawk.

Colonel Grayson records this species as very common upon the islands. Not a single individual was seen by us, and it probably occurs only as a winter visitant or stray migrant.

Falco albigularis Daudin. White-throated Falcon.

> *Hypotriorchis rufigularis* Grayson, Proc. Boston Soc. Nat. Hist., XIV, p. 269. 1871;
> Lawr., Mem. Boston Soc. Nat. Hist., II, p. 301, 1871.

Colonel Grayson took a specimen of this fine little falcon on the islands. None were seen by us, and it must, no doubt, be classed as one of the numerous accidental visitants from the mainland.

Polyborus cheriway pallidus Nelson. Tres Marias Caracara.

> *Polyborus audubonii* Grayson, Proc. Boston Soc. Nat. Hist., XIV, p. 268, 1871, (part).
> *Polyborus tharus* var. *audubonii* Lawr., Mem. Boston Soc. Nat. Hist., II, p. 303, 1874, (part).
> *Polyborus cheriway pallidus* Nelson, Proc. Biol. Soc. Washington, XII, p. 8, 1898.

Very abundant about the settlement on Maria Madre and rather commonly distributed elsewhere over the island. They were also rather common on the other islands, including San Juanito. The old log roads and dry bottoms of the canyons on Maria Madre were favorite resorts. The birds were met in many unexpected places, and were frequently seen perched in tree tops in the midst of the unbroken forest. Iguanas were excessively numerous, and furnished the main supply of food for the caracaras; the birds were on the alert, however, for anything in the form of carrion that turned up along shore or in the forest.

Pandion haliaëtus carolinensis (Gmel.) American Osprey.

Several ospreys were seen along the shores of all the islands, where they probably nest. Colonel Grayson found a nest on a rock adjacent to the northern shore of Maria Madre and another in a large cactus. Mr. Forrer obtained an immature bird during his visit to this island.

Strix pratincola Bonap. American Barn Owl.

Colonel Grayson states that he heard the well-known hissing scream of this bird at night on the Tres Marias. We were told of the presence of barn owls on the islands, but did not see them, and failed to learn whether they occur as residents or stray migrants.

Speotyto cunicularia hypogæa (Bonap.) Burrowing Owl.

Colonel Grayson says of the burrowing owl, "A few individuals of this species inhabit the Marias Islands, perhaps wandered from the m inland." We neither saw nor could learn anything of them, and those seen by Colonel Grayson were probably winter stragglers.

? Micropallas Sp.

The first evening after landing on Maria Madre, Mr. Goldman saw and heard a little owl about the size of *Glaucidium phalænoides* on an old log road in the forest. It was very near, and when he had moved back far enough to shoot without destroying the bird it became too indistinct to see and so escaped. Its notes were not like those of the ferruginous owl. This was the only one seen or heard during our stay. If a resident, it is very uncommon, for special but unsuccessful efforts were made to find others.[1]

Amazona oratrix Ridgway. Double Yellow-headed Parrot.

Chrysotis levaillantii Grayson, Proc. Boston Soc. Nat. Hist., XIV, p. 271, 1871; Lawr., Mem. Boston Soc. Nat. Hist., II, p. 296, 1874.
Amazona oratrix Ridgway, Man. N. Am. Birds, p. 594, 1887.

The yellow-headed parrot is a common resident and always nests in holes high up in large trees in the forest. Half-grown young were found the middle of May. The birds were usually seen flying about the forest in pairs, but congregated in flocks of from six to twenty or more at their feeding places. They feed upon the fruits of various trees, and during May the fleshy pods of *Pithecolobium dulce* formed their staple article of diet. These low trees, from 15 to 35 feet high, were growing around the houses of the settlement on Maria Madre and were scattered thence along the coast, especially about the borders of

---

[1] During the visit to Maria Magdalena Island a larger owl was seen in the forest along the bottom of a steep canyon, but was not sufficiently near to identify, and escaped before it could be obtained. This was probably *Ciccaba squamulata* (Bonap.), a species which is not rare on the mainland.

old clearings and in scrubby second growth on the lower slopes. A number of yellow-headed parrots came down every day to feed in the trees, even among the houses, and did not pay the slightest attention to passing people. As these birds readily learn to talk, they are highly prized as pets, and are sold to visitors, or sent to towns on the mainland; the birds taken while young being most highly prized on account of their docility. The men search for their nests, and when one is located the hunter strikes the base of the tree several sharp blows with a stone or ax, and then places his ear against the trunk and listens. He can tell whether the young are old enough to remove, by the strength of the cries they utter in reponse to the blows on the tree. Being satisfied of the presence of his game, the hunter climbs the tree, and if necessary cuts into the nest with his machete. Each brood contains two young, which are carried to the ground inside the hunter's shirt. By means of a noose on the end of a long cane, like a fishing rod, many old parrots are captured while feeding. An old woman had twenty birds which she had taken in this manner while they were feeding in the top of a small *Pithecolobium* tree by her door. The hunters search for regular feeding places in the forest and wait under the trees for the birds to come. When the birds arrive, the end of the rod is slowly and cautiously pushed up through the branches, the noose slipped over the bird's head and drawn about its neck with a quick jerk, after which the victim is hauled down and thrust into a cage. A favorite resort for the parrots on Maria Madre was a group of trees about half a mile from the settlement. The birds were very unsuspicious, and one could walk up within 20 or 25 yards in full view and watch them without their paying much attention. The parrots were constantly chattering, and the greatest good comradeship seemed to prevail. Mates kept close together and showed their attachment by caressing and feeding one another at short intervals. The proficiency in speaking which some of these birds attain is remarkable. The daughter of the customs inspector on Maria Madre had one which afforded much amusement by the variety of its remarks and their frequently absurd appropriateness. Colonel Grayson supposed these birds to be peculiar to the Tres Marias, as he did not chance to find them on the mainland. In reality, they are widely distributed on both coasts of Mexico.

After comparing the series taken on the islands with specimens from both coasts of the Mexican mainland certain slight differences are noticeable, but are too poorly defined to be worthy of subspecific recognition. The island birds are usually apple green on the dorsal surface, and mainland specimens are more of an oil green; the ventral surface has a more decided bluish wash; there is also tendency to a richer suffusion of orange and orange red on the yellow feathers about the necks of old birds.

The following measurements show that the island birds are a little larger than those of the mainland, with proportionately smaller bill and shorter tarsus. Averages of 9 specimens from the islands (both sexes): Wing, 233.3; tail, 133.6; culmen, 34.3; tarsus, 24.7. Averages of 7 specimens from both coasts of the mainland (both sexes): Wing, 222.5; tail, 120.1; culmen, 34.4; tarsus, 24.5.

Some old residents on Maria Madre reported that they had occasionally seen stray individuals of another parrot which was a little smaller than the yellow head, probably *Amazona finschi*, which is abundant on the mainland.

Psittacula insularis Ridgway. Tres Marias Lovebird.

    Psittacula cyanopyga Grayson, Proc. Boston Soc. Nat. Hist., XIV, p. 271, 1871; Lawr., Mem. Boston Soc. Nat. Hist., II, p. 297, 1874 (part).

    Psittacula insularis Ridgway, Proc. U. S. Nat. Museum, X, 1887, p. 541 (Aug. 1888).

    Psittacula cyanopygia Salvadori, Cat. Birds Brit. Mus., XX, p. 249, 1891 (part).

Lovebirds, or 'catarinas,' as they are called by the Mexicans, are common on Maria Madre and Maria Magdalena, and probably occur on Maria Cleofa, although none were seen on the latter island. They were usually seen in flocks, from a few pairs up to 30 or 40 individuals, and in May were feeding on small, sweet, wild figs, common on the lower slopes. While feeding they keep up a constant chattering, which notifies one of their presence. When flying over the top of the forest they keep in compact flocks and move steadily forward with rapid wing beats, suggesting a flock of cedar birds. They are very gentle, affectionate little creatures and quickly become tame and greatly attached to their owners.

Salvadori considers *Psittacula insularis* a synonym of *P. cyanopyga*. The series of eight adults from the islands and seven from the mainland show that the island birds can be readily distinguished. The two series show no signs of intergradation in color, and their specific distinctness is well defined, although the average measurements show but slight differences in size.

Description of Psittacula insularis, ♂ ad., Maria Madre, May, 1897:	*Description of Psittacula cyanopyga*, ♂ ad., Tepic, Mexico, April, 1897:
Cheeks, lores, forehead, and crown, back to line between orbits, rich green, decidedly clearer than in *cyanopyga*, and much more sharply contrasted with surrounding colors.	Cheeks, lores, and forehead bright green, more yellowish than in *insularis*, and shading gradually into surrounding colors.
Middle of crown green, shading abruptly into dull bluish green, which extends thence over neck, middle of back, scapulars, tertials, and lesser wing coverts.	Crown, from between orbits, neck, middle of back, scapulars, tertials, and lesser wing coverts, dark green without bluish.
Rump patch, axillars, and greater wing coverts vivid cobalt blue.	Rump patch, axillars, and greater wing coverts bright turquoise blue.
Upper tail coverts brighter green than middle of back, but darker than in *cyanopyga*.	Upper tail coverts clearer green than back.
Upper surface of tail dark green, darker than in *cyanopyga*.	Upper surface of tail rich green.

Secondaries and outer vanes of primaries near base, dark blue; primaries with outer vanes along distal half and at tips edged with dark green; inner webs of primaries brown.

Exposed under surface of primaries and secondaries dull blue.

Lower parts, back to crissum, dingy blue with a dull greenish wash; blue brightest on abdomen, and contrasting abruptly with green of crissum.

Crissum rich dark green.

Secondaries and outer vanes of inner primaries dark blue; rest of outer vanes and tips of primaries dark green; inner webs of primaries brown.

Exposed under surface of primaries and secondaries dull bluish green.

Lower parts, back to crissum, dull green, richest on abdomen and shading insensibly into color of crissum.

Crissum brighter green.

Description of Psittacula insularis, ♀ ad., Maria Madre, May, 1897.

Entire dorsal surface dingy green; brightest on sides of head, forehead, rump, and upper tail coverts, with a dull bluish shade on middle of back and wings.

Lower surface dull green, back to crissum; the latter brighter green.

Description of Psittacula cyanopyga, ♀ ad., from Tepic, Mexico, April, 1897.

Dorsal surface dark green; brightest on forehead, rump, and upper tail coverts, with an olive shade on middle of back and wings.

Lower surface nearly uniform light green, with a yellowish shade; crissum nearly the same.

Average measurements of Psittacula insularis and P. cyanopyga.

Name.	Locality.	Sex.	Number of specimens.	Wing.	Tail.	Culmen.	Tarsus.
Psittacula insularis....	Maria Madre Island........	ad. ♂	6	91.8	45.8	13.9	12.9
Psittacula insularis....	.....do................	ad. ♀	2	91.5	46.5	13.5	13
Psittacula cyanopyga..	Tepic and Jalisco..........	ad. ♂	3	90.6	45.6	12.8	13.1
Psittacula cyanopyga..	.....do................	ad. ♀	4	89.2	44.5	13.3	12.7

Coccyzus minor (Gmel.) Mangrove Cuckoo.

This bird is rather common among the mangroves and other trees bordering the salt lagoons near San Blas. A single specimen was taken on May 8 near the shore of Maria Madre, but no others were seen, and it probably occurs there only as a straggler.

Trogon ambiguus goldmani Nelson. Goldman's Trogon.

Trogon ambiguus Grayson Proc. Boston Soc. Nat. Hist., XIV, p. 272, 1871; Lawr., Mem. Boston Soc. Nat. Hist., II, p. 290, 1874 (part).
Trogon ambiguus goldmani Nelson, Proc. Biol. Soc. Washington, XII, p. 8, 1898.

Goldman's trogon was common in the more heavily wooded parts of Maria Madre and Maria Magdalena, and occurs no doubt on the less heavily wooded Cleofa. On Maria Madre they were found from the coast up nearly to the summit in suitable timber and especially along the sides and bottoms of heavily wooded canyons. Their habits were similar to those of the mainland bird. They sit quietly for a time on a branch and then fly, with an undulating motion, to another tree in the vicinity. Their notes are limited to a short succession of unmusical sounds, which are frequently heard. They were reported to nest in hollow trees. Unlike most of the birds of these islands, the trogons were nearly as shy as their representatives on the mainland. In life they have light yellow bills and bright red eyelids.

Ceryle alcyon (Linn.). Belted Kingfisher.

Colonel Grayson records that during each of his visits one or two belted kingfishers were observed sitting on rocks along the seashore. None were seen by us.

Dryobates scalaris graysoni (Baird). Grayson's Woodpecker.

Picus scalaris var. graysoni Baird, Hist. N. Am. Birds, II, pp. 515, 517, 1874; Lawr., Mem. Boston Soc. Nat. Hist., II, p. 294, 1874.

This is the only woodpecker found on the Tres Marias. It is common on all of the islands and generally distributed, except in the most heavily wooded areas. It seems to prefer second-growth thickets and other places where shrubs and scrubby trees form low and rather thin forests, and was usually seen hunting for food along the trunks of large shrubs or small trees. It was a common practice for them to alight on tree trunks near the ground and work slowly to the top, and after remaining there quietly for a time to make a short flight to another tree. Like its relative of the mainland, it is a very quiet bird, rarely uttering any call notes and making little noise while searching for food. From its habit of peering into crevices of the bark and doing only a small amount of pecking it is evident that it finds most of its food on or near the surface. Old nesting sites were seen in the trunks of both living and dead trees and in the flower stems of large magueys. The holes were usually between 5 and 10 feet from the ground. Colonel Grayson found a nest about 12 feet from the ground in the green flower stem of a large maguey (Agave) near the seashore in April.

A comparison of a series of these island woodpeckers with other forms shows that the dorsal surface, including the crest of the males, is most like typical D. scalaris from the plains of Puebla. On the ventral surface it may be distinguished from all the other races by its whiter color and scantier and smaller black markings along the sides. These markings are usually in the form of small rounded spots instead of more or less elongated streaks, as in the other races, and the white markings on the greater and lesser wing coverts are decidedly larger and more conspicuous. D. s. graysoni averages a little smaller than D. s. scalaris. The darker dorsal surface and unmarked bases of outer tail feathers distinguish it from D. s. bairdii. It has a shorter, stouter bill than D. s. lucasanus, with considerably more barring on the outer tail feathers. From D. s. sinaloensis it is distinguished mainly by its larger size, darker dorsal surface, and paler, less marked lower surface. The following averages show the relative size of *graysoni* and *sinaloensis*:

Measurements of *Dryobates s. graysoni* and *Dryobates s. sinaloensis.*

Name.	Locality.	Sex.	Number of specimens.	Wing.	Tail.	Culmen.	Tarsus.
Dryobates scalaris graysoni.	Maria Madre Island...........	ad. ♂	6	98.7	59.6	22.1	18.6
Dryobates scalaris graysoni.	.....do.....	ad. ♀	3	96.6	57	19.5	17.5
Dryobates scalaris sinaloensis.	Sinaloa and Tepic.............	ad. ♂	3	94.6	53.6	19.8	17.1

An adult female in the National Museum collection from Mazatlan, while having the normal bill and tarsus of *sinaloensis*, agrees with birds from the Tres Marias in its long wings and tail. Its measurements are as follows: Wing, 96; tail, 60; culmen, 18.5; tarsus, 16.5.

Nyctidromus albicollis insularis Nelson. Tres Marias Parauque.

   Nyctidromus albicollis Grayson, Proc. Boston Soc. Nat. Hist. XIV, p. 273, 1871;
     Lawr., Mem. Boston Soc. Nat. Hist., II, p. 291, 1874.
   Nyctidromus albicollis insularis Nelson, Proc. Biol. Soc. Washington XII, p. 9, 1898.

On the mainland the parauques are rarely seen while the sun is above the horizon, but when night falls they come out of the dense thickets where they have passed the day and sit in dusty trails and other open places. On Maria Madre they were among the commonest birds frequenting old log roads through the forest and shady canyon bottoms until late in the morning and coming out again at 3 or 4 o'clock in the afternoon. Of late years these places have been so completely given over to solitude that when a human being chances to stray into them he is looked upon with little fear. The wood folk seem to consider him harmless and only a strange creature of their own kind.

Parauques were among the most confiding birds found in these quiet retreats and permitted a close approach before taking wing and moving away. In the early dusk they were frequently seen hawking for insects among the low trees. Several came about camp at the north end of Maria Madre just after sunset, and flew very swiftly back and forth with the same erratic course and vigorous wing strokes that are so characteristic of the night-hawk. In fact, I mistook one of these birds for a night-hawk until it was secured. Their notes remind one slightly of the whip-poor-will's, but are not so loud and far-reaching. The regular call is made up of two and sometimes three syllables, besides which they have various little clucking and purring notes.

Curiously enough the parauques of the Tres Marias bear a much greater resemblance, in size and color, to *N. albicollis merrilli* of the Rio Grande Valley than to the ordinary birds of the adjacent mainland.

Chordeiles acutipennis texensis (Lawr.)   Texas Nighthawk.

A single specimen was taken May 5 on Maria Madre, and several others were seen during the first half of the mouth, after which time they disappeared. These birds were probably stray migrants, for there was nothing to indicate that they were residents.

Amazilia graysoni Lawr.   Grayson's Humming Bird.

Amazilia graysoni Lawr., Ann. Lyc. Nat. Hist., N. Y., VIII, p. 404. 1867.
Pyrrhophaena graysoni Grayson, Proc. Boston Soc. Nat. Hist., XIV, p. 283, 1871; Lawr., Mem. Boston Soc. Nat. Hist., II, p. 292, 1874.

Very common on the islands. They were seen almost everywhere darting about the less luxuriant parts of the forest hunting for flowers, and now and then stopping on a twig in some low tree top to rest or arrange their plumage. They were among the numerous feathered visitors to the little flower garden at the custom-house on Maria Madre where they were very confiding, and would carry on their search for food among the flowers quite indifferent to one's presence. These humming birds are very pugnacious, as the following incident recorded by Colonel Grayson well illustrates: "Sometimes combats between them become of a desperate nature. One day while watching a number of them in active motion around some tobacco flowers (of which they seem to be very fond) two fine males, after darting at each other for some time, at length came to a deathly struggle, high above my head; they finally clinched each other, each having one of the mandibles of the other in his mouth, at the same time scratching with their little claws, and using their wings with the greatest force, and in this situation, whirling round and round, they fell to the ground near my feet. During this terrible conflict, in which passion and desperation were exhibited, I observed them for a few seconds and then gently placed my hat over both. Even after they were thus captured, and I held one in each hand, they evidenced a desire to continue the war."

The same author records having seen these hummers dart upon and capture little flies in the manner of a flycatcher, and found their crops full of minute insects. This I can corroborate from my own observations.

Upon comparing a series of 8 specimens of *Amazilia graysoni* with an equal number of *A. cinnamomea* the general style of coloration is seen to be very similiar, yet the differences between the two forms are so constant it seems advisable to consider them specifically distinct. The dorsal surface of *A. graysoni* is a more dingy green with less coppery iridescence than in *cinnamomea;* the bronze tips of the tail feathers are less uniform, and the extreme points sometimes terminate with a little cinnamon spot; the cinnamon of the lower surface is considerably darker. There is also a well marked and constant difference in size—*graysoni* being the larger, as shown by the following averages:

Measurements of Amazilia graysoni and A. cinnamomea.

Name.	Locality.	Sex.	Number of specimens.	Wing.	Tail.	Culmen.
Amazilia graysoni	Maria Madre Island	ad. ♂	4	68.8	42.6	25
Amazilia graysoni	do	ad. ♀	4	65.9	43.4	25.4
Amazilia cinnamomea	Western Mexico	ad. ♂	7	57.9	36.6	22
Amazilia cinnamomea	do	ad. ♀	1	53	32.5	23

Iache lawrencei Ridgway. Lawrence's Humming Bird.

Circe latirostris Grayson, Proc. Boston Soc. Nat. Hist., XIV, p. 282, 1871.
Iache lawrencei (Berlepsch, Ms.) Ridgway, Man. N. Am. Birds, p. 320, 1887.

Like the preceding species this is a common and generally distributed bird, and was found on all the islands. Like Grayson's humming birds, they were common about the flower garden at the custom house on Maria Madre. Colonel Grayson found its nest on Maria Madre and describes it as follows: "The elegant little structure I found attached to a slender twig, and shaded with its leaves, about 5 feet from the ground. The situation was fronting the sea, but a few paces from the water's edge, where the first beams of the morning sun dissolved the dews. Its form is cup-shaped, and composed of the down of the silk cotton tree (*Eriodendron*) intermingled with the down of other plants and spider webs, the whole exterior neatly studded with diminutive lichens; it contained two newly hatched young, but little larger than flies."

In general appearance *Iache lawrencei* closely resembles *I. latirostris.*[1] The dorsal surfaces of the males are nearly the same color, but the upper tail coverts of *lawrencei* are grayish instead of green, as in *latirostris;* their lower surface is a darker, duller green; the blue-throat patch is nearly obsolete and replaced by an extension of the green of the neck; the under-tail coverts are darker brown.

The females of *lawrencei* differ mainly from those of *latirostris* in the clearer, brighter green of the dorsal surface and darker under-tail coverts. As the differences between the two birds seem to be fairly constant, although not very striking, it is perhaps advisable to treat them as species until more material proves the contrary.

The type of *I. latirostris* formed part of the Bullock collection and probably came from the southern end of the table-land near the Valley of Mexico. The following measurements show the differences in size:

---

[1] *Iache latirostris* undoubtedly occurs on the islands as a straggler. About midway on our return to the coast a hummer passed close to the side of the boat, coming from the direction of San Blas and heading in a direct line for the islands. As this wanderer passed I had a close view and identified it as *I. latirostris.*

Measurements of Iache lawrencei and I. latirostris.

Name.	Locality.	Sex.	Number of specimens.	Wing.	Tail.	Culmen.
Iache lawrencei	Maria Madre Island	ad. ♂	3	52.3	32.6	18.8
Iache lawrencei	do	ad. ♀	4	51.2	29.2	20.2
Iache latirostris	Southern table-lands, Mexico	ad. ♂	5	54.2	33	21.9
Iache latirostris	do	ad. ♀	1	52	33	23

Platypsaris aglaiæ insularis (Ridg.) Grayson's Becard.

> *Hadrostomus aglaiæ* var. *affinis* Grayson, Proc. Boston Soc. Nat. Hist., XIV, p. 279, 1871; Lawr., Mem. Boston Soc. Nat. Hist., II, p. 289, 1874.
>
> *Platypsaris insularis* Ridgway, Man. N. Am. Birds, p. 325, 1887.

The rose-throated becard was not common and only three specimens were taken, all on Maria Madre. They were found in the heavier forest on the slopes well back from the coast, and nothing unusual was noted in regard to their habits. They probably occur on Maria Magdalena and perhaps on Maria Cleofa. A considerable series of specimens from various parts of Mexico shows that a single species of rose-breasted becard ranges over a large part of Mexico and has developed four geographical subspecies. The ranges of these four forms may be defined as follows:

Platypsaris aglaiæ (Lafr.). Eastern Mexico from northern Tamaulipas south along basal slopes of the Cordillera of Vera Cruz and Tabasco to arid parts of Yucatan. (Type from vicinity of Jalapa, Vera Cruz.)

Platypsaris aglaiæ sumichrasti Nelson. Humid lowlands of Vera Cruz, and thence southward in similar country nearly or quite to Guatemala. (Type from Otatitlan, Vera Cruz.)

Platypsaris aglaiæ albiventris (Lawr.). West coast of Mexico from the Isthmus of Tehauntepec to southern Arizona, ranging along river valleys into the interior of western Mexico. (Type from Plains of Colima.)

Platypsaris aglaiæ insularis (Ridg.). Tres Marias Islands. (Type from Maria Madre Island.)

Typical specimens of *insularis* are much darker than typical examples of *albiventris*. Specimens from the coast lowlands about San Blas are intermediate in color. The island birds, however, may usually be distinguished by their smaller bills. Back from the coast of Tepic, especially in the arid river canyons at Bolaños and near Guadalajara, only typical specimens of *albiventris* were found. On the eastern side of Mexico these two forms are paralleled by the pale bird of the foot hills and adjacent interior (*aglaiæ*) and the darker one of the coast lowlands (*sumichrasti*). The color of extreme specimens of *albiventris* is very different from that of *aglaiæ* and *insularis*, but among the series from western Mexico, where *albiventris* has its home, are various intermediate stages, some specimens approaching very closely to both the forms just named. Some specimens of *insularis* are much nearer typical *aglaiæ* in color than *albiventris*. Females of *insularis* are more distinct from those of *aglaiæ* than the males, owing to their generally grayer backs, but even this is not a constant character. The only character of *insularis* that is fairly constant is the smaller bill; a curious development, since there is a general tendency to an increase in size of bill among Tres Marias birds.

Measurements of Platypsaris aglaiæ and its races in Mexico.

Name.	Locality.	Sex.	Number of specimens.	Wing.	Tail.	Culmen.	Tarsus.
Platypsaris aglaiæ...	Eastern Mexico	ad. ♂	3	94.3	72.3	16	21.8
Platypsaris aglaiæ sumichrasti.	Otatitlan, Vera Cruz	ad. ♂	3	89.6	68.3	16.3	22
Platypsaris aglaiæ albiventris.	Plains of Colima and Bolaños, Jalisco.	ad. ♂	4	90.5	67.5	15.8	21.6
Platypsaris aglaiæ insularis.	Maria Madre Island...........	ad. ♂	3	87	66.8	14.3	22.1
Platypsaris aglaiæ insularis.	.....do.....................	ad. ♀	3	88	66.6	15	22.3
Intermediates between P. a. albiventris and P. a. insularis.	Coast near San Blas, Tepic....	ad. ♂	3	89.8	64.3	15.3	22.3

Tyrannus melancholicus couchi (Baird.)   Couch's Kingbird.

On Maria Madre Island ten or a dozen of these birds were seen and appeared to be resident. Two or three were noted on Maria Magdalena, and others on Maria Cleofa, where they were most numerous. They were always found near the seashore. The specimens obtained seem to be identical with those from the adjacent mainland. As a rule birds from northeastern Mexico, the type locality, are lighter than those from western Mexico, but this difference is not constant.

Myiarchus mexicanus magister Ridgway.   Arizona Crested Flycatcher.

Although resident on all the islands, birds from the Tres Marias are almost identical with those from the mainland, and nothing distinctive was noted in their habits. They frequent the thinner parts of the scrubby forests which cover most of the slopes, but were most numerous within a mile or two of the sea. They kept among the low trees, usually perching on tops of bushes or on branches within 10 or 15 feet of the ground, where they watched for passing insects.

Myiarchus lawrencei olivascens Ridgway.   Olivaceous Flycatcher.

This was much more abundant than the preceding species, and one of the commonest and most generally distributed resident birds on the islands. Like the preceding, it was most numerous in the scrubby forest within a mile or two of the seashore and kept among the branches of trees and bushes within 10 or 15 feet of the ground. Its habits were the same as on the mainland.

A careful comparison of series from the islands and the mainland shows but little difference. The island birds are slightly grayer on the back, the bills average a little longer and wider, and the tarsus is longer, but these differences are too slight to warrant subspecific recognition. Unfortunately the type of this subspecies is based on a winter specimen from Santa Efigenia, Oaxaca, near the border of Chiapas. This leaves the summer range of typical birds in doubt.

Below are averages of specimens from the islands and the mainland:

Measurements of Myiarchus lawrencei olivascens.

Name.	Locality	Sex.	Number of specimens.	Wing.	Tail.	Culmen.	Tarsus
Myiarchus lawrencei olivascens.	Tres Marias Islands	ad. ♀	7	76.3	74.8	16.8	19.7
Myiarchus lawrencei olivascens.	Northwest Mexico, southern Arizona	ad. ♀	7	76.8	74.7	16.1	18.8

Contopus richardsonii (Swains). Western Wood Pewee.

During the first ten days of May these birds were not uncommon in some of the denser growths of small trees along the lower slopes of Maria Madre. None were seen on the other islands and they all disappeared a little later, showing that they were merely stray migrants. The single specimen taken is identical with others from the western United States.

Empidonax difficilis Baird. Western Flycatcher.

These birds were very sparingly distributed on the Tres Marias. They were seen on Maria Madre soon after our arrival, and on May 27 one was taken on Maria Magdalena. They were usually found in dense thickets and along shady canyons. Colonel Grayson records them as common, but they undoubtedly occur only as winter visitants and migrants.

Ornithion imberbe (Sclater). Beardless Flycatcher.

Two specimens were taken and a few others seen early in May on Maria Madre; none were seen later, and they probably occur merely as stragglers during migration. They move about like small vireos in the tops of low trees and in large bushes, searching the outer twigs for insects and flying out every now and then to capture one on the wing.

A series of specimens from various localities on both coasts and the interior of Mexico, the Tres Marias Islands, and southern Arizona fails to show any tangible characters to distinguish *O. imberbe ridgwayi* from typical *O. imberbe*.

13950—No. 14——4

Myiopagis placens (Sclater). Golden Crowned Flycatcher.

In the National Museum collection is a typical specimen of *M. placens*, taken by Colonel Grayson in January, 1865, on the Tres Marias Islands, which agrees perfectly in size and color with the large dark birds from the mountains of Jalisco, on the adjacent mainland. Eight specimens of both sexes from various localities in Mexico and Central America average as follows: Wing, 68.2; tail, 65.8; culmen, 11.2; tarsus, 19.1.

Myiopagis placens minimus Nelson. Little Golden Crowned Flycatcher.

  Elainea placens Lawr., Proc. Boston Soc. Nat. Hist., XIV, p. 279, 1871; Mem. Boston Soc. Nat. Hist., II, p. 286, 1874.
  Myiopagis placens minimus Nelson, Proc. Biol. Soc. Washington, XII, p. 9, 1898.

Early in May a few of these birds were seen in the low scrubby forest near the shore on Maria Madre, but by the middle of the month they had retired to the heavily wooded canyons and slopes above 600 or 800 feet. They were common among the trees bordering the head of a large canyon in the middle of the island, where a small spring formed the center of attraction for many birds. Like their mainland relative, they frequent the tree tops, where they may be seen running in and out among the ends of the branches and fluttering about the tips of twigs in the manner of some warblers. They frequently hop from twig to twig, with their tails uptilted like gnatcatchers, but their dull garb is usually sufficient to identify them. When high up in the tops of tall trees, however, their form and habits are so warbler-like that they can not be distinguished from other small birds. A few individuals were seen on Maria Magdalena, but none on Maria Cleofa.

Corvus mexicanus Gmelin. Mexican Crow.

Two residents on Maria Madre reported that at long intervals they had seen stray crows on the island. My informants were familiar with the bird on the mainland, where it is extremely numerous about San Blas, and there is no reason to doubt the correctness of their identification.

Cissolopha beecheyi (Vigors). Beechey's Jay.

A specimen of this bird in the National Museum collection, obtained by Xantus, is labeled "Tres Marias Islands, October 15, 1859". This record, however, is doubtful.

Icterus graysoni Cassin. Grayson's Oriole.

  Icterus graysoni Cassin, Proc. Acad. Nat. Sci. Phila., p. 48, 1867; Mem. Boston Soc. Nat. Hist., II, p. 280, 1874.

These beautiful birds are very common on all of the islands. Although more numerous about the settlement on Maria Madre than elsewhere, they were common in the thin, low forest all about the lower parts of the islands and were very unsuspicious. During my excursions through the woods they came again and again and alighted on low branches of shrubs or trees beside the old log roads and peered at me with innocently inquiring eyes as if wondering at the strange creature newly arrived in their haunts, but evidently quite unconscious of any feeling that the newcomer might be dangerous. Such confidence made it very trying work to collect many of these birds.

They came familiarly about the houses and yards at the settlement on Maria Madre. A number of them made several visits each day to the verandas and shrubbery about the custom-house, and added greatly to the attractive surroundings by their bright colors and frank unconcern. They searched for insects among the shrubs and small trees in the patio or court, came to the veranda railing, down upon the floor, and along the walls, where plump spiders furnished many choice morsels. Several bags of corn piled against the wall on one side of the veranda were infested with weevils, which could be found creeping about on the outside of the bags. A pair of orioles was in the habit of regularly visiting the veranda and soon discovered these insects. They walked all over the bags, sometimes upside down or on one side like a nuthatch, and pried into every spot likely to contain a little beetle. They were frequently seen also clinging to the stems of the giant cactus (*Cereus*) and feeding on the juicy fruit.

As Colonel Grayson has recorded, the nests of these orioles are about a foot in length and of the usual purse shape. They are made of fibers of grass or maguey plants, lined with silk cotton and swung near the end of some slender branch overhanging a clear space, usually from 18 to 35 feet above the ground.

Grayson's oriole is evidently an offshoot from the wide ranging *Icterus pustulatus* of the adjacent coast, but has become sufficiently distinct to rank as a species. Like so many of the island birds, it is larger than its mainland relative. The yellow is much lighter than on *I. pustulatus* and lacks most of the intense orange that is so conspicuous on many of the latter birds. Some adult males of *graysoni* have the back entirely bright yellow, while the backs of others are marked with a few narrow black shaft streaks. The females of *graysoni* are more greenish-yellow and have but faint traces of the orange shade present in typical *pustulatus*.

The following averages show the relative dimensions of the two species:

Measurements of Icterus graysoni and I. pustulatus.

Name.	Locality.	Sex.	Number of specimens.	Wing.	Tail.	Culmen.	Tarsus.
Icterus graysoni	Maria Madre Island	ad. ♂	4	104	89.7	25.4	26.7
Icterus graysoni	do	ad. ♀	4	96.7	84.2	25.1	26.2
Icterus pustulatus	Western Mexico	ad. ♂	4	100.2	91	21	25.6
Icterus pustulatus	do	ad. ♀	4	91.7	81.5	20.2	24.5

Quiscalus macrourus Swainson. Great-tailed Grackle.

Two of these grackles were shot the latter part of May on a level bit of ground bordering the shore in front of the settlement on Maria Madre. They were the only ones seen and were undoubtedly stragglers from the mainland where they are abundant and resident near San Blas.

Astragalinus psaltria mexicanus (Swainson). Mexican Goldfinch.

Rather common and apparently resident, but nothing distinctive was observed in their habits. On Maria Madre they were usually found on the lower slopes and were most numerous about the settlement. Ten specimens fail to show any characters distinguishing the island birds from those of the mainland.

Cardinalis cardinalis mariæ Nelson. Tres Marias Cardinal.

Cardinalis virginianus Lawr., Proc. Boston Soc. Nat. Hist., XIV, p. 281, 1871.

Cardinalis virginianus var. *igneus* Lawr., Mem. Boston Soc. Nat. Hist., II, p. 275, 1874.

Cardinalis cardinalis mariæ Nelson, Proc. Biol. Soc. Washington, XII, p. 10, 1898.

Cardinals were very common on Maria Madre and not uncommon on the rest of the group. No one ever molests them, and they were especially abundant about the settlement, where they came into the yards and around the houses in the most familiar way. Several pairs could be found at any time during a short walk in the scrubby thickets along the lower slopes of the island. While we were hunting in the low woods it was a common occurrence for them to come very near, and after looking at the intruders with mild curiosity for a short time, to move off through the bushes in quiet pursuit of their usual occupations. At other times, while engaged in search of food among the fallen leaves they would scarcely notice one as he walked slowly by within three or four paces.

Piranga ludoviciana (Wilson). Louisiana Tanager.

During the first half of May these tanagers were not uncommon near the settlement on Maria Madre, but were not seen on the other islands. Those shot the first of the month were in fair condition, and, several pairs being seen, it was at first considered a resident species. Later, when others were secured, it was noted that they were more and more emaciated, until those killed about the middle of the month were so excessively thin, it was surprising that they had continued to live. About this time the last ones disappeared, no doubt dying from starvation. From these observations it appeared that the birds must have strayed to the island during migration, about the last of April or first of May, and were unable to find a proper food supply. At the same time they feared to start over the sea for an invisible shore and so perished. Another member of the genus, *Piranga bidentata flammea*, is resident in large numbers on the islands and found an abundant food supply, as was shown by their being among the fattest birds collected during the time that *P. ludoviciana* was dying of starvation.

Piranga bidentata flammea (Ridgway). Tres Marias Tanager.

Pyranga bidentata Lawr., Proc. Boston Soc. Nat. Hist., XIV, p. 281, 1871; Mem. Boston Soc. Nat. Hist., II, p. 274 (part), 1874.

Piranga flammea Ridgway, Man. N. Am. Birds, p. 457, 1887.

Several species of birds were very much at home about the settlement on Maria Madre, and among these the brilliant Tres Marias tanager was one of the most numerous. Like Grayson's oriole, they came daily to the veranda railing and investigated the shrubs and small trees in the court and flower garden at the custom-house. These birds were common and generally distributed in the scrubby forest on the lower parts of Maria Madre and Maria Magdalena, and probably occur on Maria Cleofa, although none were seen there. Their habits were very much like those of *Piranga bidentata* on the mainland. On the island, however, these tanagers were most numerous within a few hundred feet of sea level, while their relatives of the mainland inhabited oak forests at an altitude of 2,000 or 3,000 feet. They have a short warbling song, which is similar to, but less musical than, that of the mainland bird. They were seen hunting for food in the small tree tops of the scantier forest growths rather than in the more densely wooded areas and were very fat.

P. bidentata was described by Swainson from a specimen in the Bullock collection, taken at Temascaltepec, southwest of the Valley of Mexico, on the Pacific slope of the mountains. It was described as having the 'head, neck, and under parts golden'. This style of coloration is shown in specimens from various localities in Jalisco, Sinaloa, and the Tres Marias Islands. Judging from specimens in the National Museum and from the results of recent work, tanagers of this description are only found north of the Isthmus of Tehuantepec, on the arid western slope of Mexico, and are not common. The Tres Marias tanager is closely related to typical *P. bidentata*, and the males are so closely alike in color that it requires careful scrutiny to find distinguishing characters. In *P. flammea* the white tips of the greater and lesser wing coverts are larger and clearer white than in *P. bidentata*, thus rendering the two wing bands more conspicuous. The white spots on the outer rectrices are smaller and confined to the inner webs, except at the extreme tip; in *P. bidentata* these marks occupy most of the terminal third of the feathers. In general color of the body the two forms are indistinguishable. The bill of *P. flammea* averages longer and is decidedly more swollen, especially toward the tip; this difference is one of the most important characters of the island form. The female of *P. flammea* can be distinguished only by the larger bill and the restriction of the white spot on the outer pair of tail feathers.

The following measurements give the averages of the two forms:

Measurements of Piranga bidentata and Piranga b. flammea.

Name.	Locality.	Sex.	Number of specimens.	Wing.	Tail.	Culmen.	Tarsus.
Piranga bidentata flammea.	Maria Madre Island..	ad. ♂	6	94	81	18.1	23.7
Piranga bidentata flammea.	....do	ad. ♀	4	95	78.7	18.4	22.5
Piranga bidentata..........	Jalisco and Sinaloa...	ad. ♂	3	98	79.3	17.3	21.1
Piranga bidentata..........	....do	ad. ♀	2	96	79	17	21.5

Hirundo erythrogaster Bodd. Barn Swallow.

Soon after our arrival on Maria Madre a few swallows, supposed to be this species, were seen by my assistant, but none were taken. They were undoubtedly stray migrants, for none were seen afterwards.

Vireo flavoviridis forreri (Madarasz). Forrer's Vireo.

Vireo forreri Madarász, Természetrajzi Füzetek, IX, pt. 1, p. 85, 1885.

Although Forrer's vireo is one of the most abundant and widely distributed species on the islands, yet it does not appear in Grayson's list. It was very common in the small trees in the patio of the customhouse and elsewhere about the settlement on Maria Madre. Like its mainland relative, its habits are very similar to those of the red-eyed vireo. Its favorite range was in the smaller growth of forest along the lower slopes, from near the sea up to an altitude of 600 or 700 feet, but some were seen up near the summits of Maria Madre and Maria Magdalena. Next to the Tres Marias warbler, Forrer's vireo was probably the most abundant bird on Maria Madre, and its restless habits while fluttering and peering about in search of food among the small tree tops added greatly to the animation of the forest.

Vireo forreri is evidently only a geographical race of *Vireo flavoviridis*. It has the same color pattern, but the ashy crown is paler and the dusky supraorbital stripe usually obsolescent; the latter is one of the main characters upon which *forreri* was originally based, but is not constant. Some specimens from the islands have this stripe as strongly marked as dull-colored individuals of *flavoviridis* proper, although none have it so strongly marked as some of the latter. The two forms are alike on the underparts, and the greater size of *forreri* is the most constant and striking character.

Average measurements of 17 adult males of *Vireo flavoviridis forreri*: Wing, 84.3; tail, 59.3; culmen, 15.1; tarsus, 20.1. Averages of *Vireo flavoviridis* (from mainland of Mexico): Ad. ♂ (9 specimens), wing, 79.2; tail, 55.1; culmen, 14.3; tarsus, 18.7. Ad. ♀ (3 specimens), wing, 76.6; tail, 50.6; culmen, 14.1; tarsus, 18.5.

Vireo hypochryseus sordidus Nelson. Tres Marias Vireo.

Vireo hypochryseus Grayson, Proc. Boston Soc. Nat. Hist., XIV, p. 281, 1871; Lawr., Mem. Boston Soc. Nat. Hist., II, p. 272, 1874.

Vireo hypochryseus sordidus Nelson. Proc. Biol. Soc. Washington, XII, p. 10, 1898.

A few of these vireos were seen in the thin forest on the lower slopes of Maria Madre, but were not common. They were especially numerous among the trees and tall bushes about the few springs and little streams near the summit. A few were also seen in similar places on Maria Magdalena. *Vireo f. forreri* occupies the lower slopes, while *sordidus* occurs mainly higher up, the ranges of the two birds being complementary. The Tres Marias vireo is usually found at a medium height among the foliage of thick-topped trees, rarely ascending to the extreme top. It was also often seen in the dense, tall undergrowth near water.

Compsothlypis insularis (Lawr.). Tres Marias Parula.

> *Parula insularis* Lawr., Ann. Lyc. Nat. Hist., N. Y., X, p. 4, 1871; Grayson, Proc. Boston Soc. Nat. Hist., XIV, pp. 278, 300, 1871; Lawr., Mem. Boston Soc. Nat. Hist., II, p. 269, 1874.

These pretty little warblers were the most abundant of the land birds on the Tres Marias. A few of them were also found on Isabel Island, and the only *Compsothlypis* taken on the mainland at San Blas belongs to this species. They frequent the thin forest of the lower slopes on the Tres Marias, and dozens of them were seen during every visit to the woods, and they were seen in smaller numbers on the higher slopes. Many also came familiarly into the small trees and shrubbery about the houses at the settlement. They were always busily at work in pursuit of insects among the branches, and searched the bark of small shrubs near the ground as well as the branches at the tops of large trees. They were rather common in the scrubby growth of stunted trees on Isabel, and were very abundant in the tree tops of the heavy forest on the mainland between San Blas and Santiago. Their song is weak and lisping and not at all musical.

There is little doubt that a good series of specimens will demonstrate that *Compsothlypis pitiayumi* of northern South America is represented in Central America and Mexico by a number of geographical races rather than by the closely related species now recognized—*C. inornata*, *C. pulchra*, *C. nigrilora*, and *C. insularis*. Even the imperfect series at hand shows signs of intergradation, but treating *C. insularis* as a species for the present, its differences from its nearest relative, *C. pulchra*, are set forth in the following notes. *C. pulchra* was the only form found on the mainland back of the low coast plain on the tropical or subtropical slopes of the mountains. This species was described from Chihuahua, and appears to be a resident of the lower slopes of the Sierra Madre, ranging from Chihuahua to Tepic, while *C. insularis* is characteristic of the hot lowlands on the coast near San Blas and the outlying islands.

C. insularis is larger than *C. pulchra*, with a heavier shading of brown along the flanks; the yellow of the under parts is duller and more generally suffused with dull orange brown; the white spots on outer tail feathers are decidedly larger, and the bluish of the dorsal surface is grayer. In the small series examined, difference in size seems to be the most constant character. Following are average measurements of the two species:

Measurements of Compsothlypis insularis and C. pulchra.

Name.	Locality.	Sex.	Number of specimens.	Wing.	Tail.	Culmen.	Tarsus.
Compsothlypis insularis ...	Maria Madre Island ..	ad. ♂	6	60	49.3	10.4	19.9
Compsothlypis insularis ...	...do	ad. ♀	4	55.7	47.5	10	19
Compsothlypis pulchra.....	Jalisco and Sinaloa ...	ad. ♂	3	55.6	42.3	9.6	17
Compsothlypis pulchra....	...do	ad. ♀	1	52	41	1	17

Dendroica æstiva rubiginosa (Pallas). Alaskan Yellow Warbler.

Several of these birds were taken and others seen about the settlement on Maria Madre. They were evidently stray migrants, and most of them left before the end of May.

Dendroica æstiva morcomi Coale. Western Yellow Warbler.

Among the yellow warblers taken on Maria Madre during the first half of May were two specimens referable to *Dendroica æstiva morcomi*. Like *rubiginosa*, they were stray migrants which had wandered out of their course while en route to their more northern breeding grounds. They were found about weed patches and shrubbery in the settlement.

Dendroica auduboni (Townsend). Audubon's Warbler.

Two of these birds were seen during the first half of May about the settlement on Maria Madre, and May 30 a specimen was taken on Maria Cleofa. Like the yellow warblers, they occur merely as stray migrants and were seen only near the seashore.

Dendroica townsendii (Townsend). Townsend's Warbler.

Two or three of these warblers were seen at the settlement on Maria Madre between the 8th and 20th of May. They kept about the weed patches and yards for several days, and were stray migrants like the preceding species.

Granatellus francescæ Baird. Tres Marias Chat-Warbler.

> *Granatellus francesca* Bair l. Rev. Am. Birds, p. 232, 1865; Grayson, Proc. Boston Soc. Nat. Hist., XIV, p. 278, 1871; Lawr., Mem. Boston Soc. Nat. Hist., II, p. 270, 1874.

These beautiful birds were seen only on Maria Madre, but they probably occur also on Maria Magdalena, where the conditions are equally favorable. They were far from common, and inhabited the forest on the higher slopes, but two or three individuals, evidently wanderers, were encountered in the scrubby forest near the shore. They were usually seen on the ground searching for food among low underbrush and weeds. In such places they ran about among the thick stems of plants and matted undergrowth, springing up every now and then to a twig or weed stalk a foot or two from the ground, and then perhaps flitting along from stem to stem to another feeding place a few yards away. When thus passing through the undergrowth, they are very conspicuous and attractive objects, owing to their beautifully contrasted black, white, and rose-colored plumage. Their habit of carrying the tail up-tilted and more or less widely spread renders them still more conspicuous. It is doubtful if they ascend into the tops of trees, as they are even more terrestrial than their relatives the chats.

The color pattern of this species is much like that of *G. venustus*, but the black collar on the lower side of the neck in the males is nearly obsolete, being represented only by a few black feathers, the red or rose colored area on the breast and chest is paler and more restricted, the postocular white stripe larger and extending across the nape as an indistinct nuchal band, the bluish of the dorsal surface grayer, and the white on the tail more extended. The females are browner above and paler below. *G. francesca* is larger than *G. venustus*, as shown by the following averages:

Measurements of Granatellus francesca and G. venustus.

Name.	Locality.	Sex.	Number of specimens.	Wing.	Tail.	Culmen.	Tarsus.
Granatellus francesca	Maria Madre Island	ad. ♂	5	65.8	76.5	12.2	21
Granatellus francesca	do	ad. ♀	2	63	74.5	12.2	21.5
Granatellus venustus	Guerrero and Oaxaca	ad. ♂	2	61.5	66.5	12	19.7
Granatellus venustus	do	ad. ♀	1	58	67	12	20.5

Wilsonia pusilla pileolata (Pall.). Pileolated Warbler.

The only one seen was taken on Maria Cleofa May 30. It was in some bushes by a little stream near the seashore and was evidently a straggling migrant.

Mimus polyglottos (Linn.). Mocking Bird.

A few mocking birds were seen on Maria Madre, where they are probably resident in small numbers. They were found only on the lower slopes near the sea. The two specimens secured appear to be identical with others from the adjacent mainland.

Thryothorus lawrencii (Ridgway). Maria Madre Wren.

Thryothorus felix Grayson, Proc. Boston Soc. Nat. Hist. XIV, p. 278, 1871 (part);
Lawr., Mem. Boston Soc. Nat. Hist. II, p. 268, 1874 (part).
Thryothorus felix β lawrencii Ridgway, Bull. Nutt. Orn. Club, III, p. 10, Jan., 1878.

The song of this wren was one of the most constant and pleasing of the woodland notes heard on Maria Madre. The bird was extremely abundant everywhere in the undergrowth ranging from the shore up to the higher slopes. Like its near relatives, it is a restless little creature, constantly climbing and peering about in the thickets. The male stops every now and then to utter his song and then continues insect hunting. When in a musical mood he takes a position in some small shrub, sometimes on its summit but oftener on a branch at one side, and there pours out his song again and again at short intervals. Like many other birds on these islands, the wren was very familiar and unsuspicious, and many came every day to the fences and shrubbery around the houses at the settlement.

A series of *Thryothorus felix* from the mainland, including one specimen from the region of the type locality, and a series of *T. lawrencii* from Maria Madre, show sufficient differences to warrant giving specific rank to *lawrencii*. The latter differs very constantly in several respects from birds of the mainland, but has much the same color pattern. The series from San Blas is nearer *lawrencii* than is the specimen from near the type locality of *felix*, but there appears to be no crossing of the gap between the two.

The following measurements show the relative sizes of the two species:

Measurements of Thryothorus lawrencii and T. felix.

Name.	Locality.	Sex.	Number of specimens.	Wing.	Tail.	Culmen.	Tarsus.
Thryothorus lawrencii ...	Maria Madre Island...	ad. ♂	3	60	55.6	17.2	22
Thryothorus lawrencii.....	....do	ad. ♀	7	57.1	54	16.8	21.4
Thryothorus felix..........	Santiago, Teplo to Ometepec, Guerrero.	ad. ♂	2	57.5	55.5	16	21.5
Thryothorus felix..........	....do	ad. ♀	3	54.3	50.6	14.6	20.5

Thryothorus lawrencii magdalenæ Nelson. Magdalena Wren.

> *Thryothorus felix* Grayson Proc. Boston Soc. Nat. Hist., XIV, p. 278, 1871 (part); Lawr., Mem. Boston Soc. Nat. Hist., II, p. 268, 1874 (part).
> *Thryothorus lawrencii magdalenæ* Nelson, Proc. Biol. Soc. Washington, XII, p. 11, 1898.

The habits and distribution of this wren on Maria Magdalena are the same as those of *T. lawrencii* on Maria Madre. No one lives on Maria Magdalena, and the wrens are even tamer than on Maria Madre. Their confidence was shown very prettily by one encountered by Mr. Goldman in the dark bottom of a narrow rocky canyon overhung with heavy forest. He saw the little fellow busily searching for food among the fallen leaves along the base of a low cliff, and as the bird seemed very fearless he approached quietly but in full view, and succeeded in closing his hand over the tiny creature, which had continued its search without paying the slightest attention. The bird showed but little fright, and its captor, after holding it a few moments, stooped and gently opened his hand to let it escape. The wren hopped away a few feet, arranged its plumage, and then continued feeding with the utmost unconcern. Mr. Goldman watched it for a few minutes and again approached slowly. As before the bird paid no attention until he was within a yard, but when another attempt was made to pick it up, hopped away a few feet and again resumed its occupation. This was repeated three or four times with the same result, until finally the bird was left in its solitude.

Melanotis cærulescens longirostris Nelson. Tres Marias Blue Mockingbird.

Melanotis cærulescens Grayson Proc. Boston Soc. Nat. Hist., XIV, p. 275, 1871; Lawr., Mem. Boston Soc. Nat. Hist., II, p. 266, 1874 (part).

Melanotis cærulescens longirostris Nelson, Proc. Biol. Soc. Washington, XII, p. 10 1898.

These fine songsters are very common on the Tres Marias. They keep in the thickets and low trees and bushes like a catbird and were especially numerous and familiar about the settlement on Maria Madre. In one yard, among a few fruit trees, a trough was kept full of water, where scores of blue mockingbirds came daily to drink and would almost allow themselves to be caught by hand. Their numbers and general distribution make them among the most noticeable birds on the islands, and they frequently follow one with much curiosity. Their song, although rich and varied, was not so clear and musical as that of their relatives on the mainland. The birds on Maria Madre show a marked tendency to albinism, which usually appears in the form of grayish or whitish bars on the wings and tail. In addition to the barring on the primaries and secondaries, the alula is often similarly marked and some specimens have lighter spots on the tips of the wing coverts, producing well-defined wing bands. The markings are usually symmetrical, but vary in amount and intensity with the individual. In some they are barely distinguishable and in others very conspicuous. More rarely the albinism appears on other parts of the body, occasionally in asymmetrical areas of pure white, but these spots also are sometimes regular. One specimen has the entire under surface white, except some blue feathers along the flanks, and the rump is white mixed with blue. This bird has a striking general resemblance to the Central American *Melanotis hypoleucus*. At least 2 or 3 per cent of the birds on the islands are albinistic, and the constant recurrence of the same light barring on the wings and tail seems to indicate the possible evolution of a form in which these markings will be constant.

Myadestes obscurus insularis Stejneger. Tres Marias Solitaire.

Myiadestes obscurus Grayson, Proc. Boston Soc. Nat. Hist., XIV, p. 277, 1871; Lawr., Mem. Boston Soc. Nat. Hist., II, p. 273, 1874.

Myadestes obscurus var. *insularis* Stejneger, Proc. U. S. Nat. Mus., IV, pp. 371, 373, 1882.

This is a common bird in the heavy forest about the heads of canyons on Maria Madre and Maria Magdalena. They were not found anywhere in the scrubby growth of the lower slopes, and if they occur there at all it must be only as stragglers. They are shy birds, remaining silent when approached, but when undisturbed flitting through the tree tops like wandering spirits of melody uttering their sweet strains from the mysterious depths of the forest. Their song was heard from the tops of tall trees where the birds sat amid the heavy foliage, rarely coming down to lower levels except in the morning or evening, or to drink at midday. Many were seen about a spring near the top of Maria Madre where they came to drink at noon.

Although *Myadestes obscurus insularis* is very closely related to *occidentalis*, yet it may be distinguished by several slight but constant characters, such as the greater extension and paler shade of ashy from the neck over the forward part of the back. The lower parts also are paler, especially on the throat and abdomen. The white tips to the tail feathers, mentioned by Dr. Stejneger as characteristic of this form, are equally common on specimens of *occidentalis*.

The following measurements show the relative size of the two forms:

Measurements of Myadestes obscurus insularis and Myadestes o. occidentalis.

Name.	Locality.	Sex.	Number of specimens.	Wing.	Tail.	Culmen.	Tarsus.
Myadestes obscurus insularis.	Maria Madre Island ..	ad. ♂	5	102.7	102.6	12.2	22.5
Myadestes obscurus insularis.	.....do	ad. ♀	3	98.6	95.6	11.5	22
Myadestes obscurus occidentalis.	Jalisco and Sinaloa ...	ad. ♂	3	104	102.3	12.5	22.1
Myadestes obscurus occidentalis.	.....do	ad. ♀	2	100.5	92	12	21.7

Hylocichla ustulata (Nuttall). Russet-backed Thrush.

A typical specimen of this species, taken on the islands by Colonel Grayson in the winter of 1865, is in the National Museum. In his notes Colonel Grayson says: "I found this little thrush in the month of January quite abundant in the thickest of the woods of the Tres Marias. It is very timid and shy, more so than any bird I saw upon the islands; it frequently uttered a low, plaintive whistle, and seemed solitary in its habits." We saw none of them on the islands in May, and it is safe to class them as winter visitants.

Hylocichla ustulata swainsonii (Cabanis). Olive-backed Thrush.
   Hylocichla ustulata almæ Oberholser, Auk, XV, p. 304, October, 1898.

Two specimens of this thrush were taken on Marie Madre, one on May 5, the other on May 19. They were found in the heavy forest back from the coast, and evidently occur only as stray migrants.

Mr. Oberholser mentions these specimens as typical examples of his subspecies, which is considered a synonym of *Hylocichla u. swainsonii* by the American Ornithologists' Union.

Merula graysoni Ridgway. Tres Marias Robin.
   Turdus flavirostris Grayson, Proc. Boston Soc. Nat. Hist., XIV, p. 276, 1871 (part);
      Lawr., Mem. Boston Soc. Nat. Hist., II, p. 266, 1874 (part);
   Merula flavirostris graysoni Ridgway, Proc. U. S. Nat. Mus., V, p. 12, 1882.

Grayson's robin is one of the most abundant and widely spread residents and takes the place of *M. flavirostris* of the mainland, which it closely resembles in habits and general appearance. Although a characteristic bird of the islands, yet occasional stragglers reach the mainland, as is shown by a perfectly typical specimen (a female in worn plumage) taken at Santiago, Territory of Tepic, June 20, 1897. On the islands it was found from the shore to the forests of the higher slopes and was also very plentiful and familiar about the settlement. It had a variety of notes, among them a rich warbling song and a characteristic clear, mellow, whistling call. While among the trees, or during their search for food upon the ground, these birds closely resemble the common robin in habits and general appearance. At the time of our visit a species of wild fig was in fruit, and the tops of the trees were swarming with these robins, tanagers, orioles, lovebirds, and trogons, all eagerly feeding upon the figs.

Merula graysoni is another of the Tres Marias birds which are evidently offshoots from species now resident on the adjacent mainland, but with differences sufficiently pronounced and constant to warrant their recognition as separate species. *Merula flavirostris*, the mainland representative of the Tres Marias robin, is much more richly colored than *graysoni*, and the differences mentioned by Mr. Ridgway are constant and well shown in the present series. The following average measurements show the relative dimensions of the two species:

Measurements of Merula graysoni and M. flavirostris.

Name.	Locality.	Sex.	Number of specimens.	Wing.	Tail.	Culmen.	Tarsus.
Merula graysoni	Maria Madre Island	ad. ♂	4	127	99.7	24.4	34.5
Merula graysoni	do	ad. ♀	5	125.6	98.8	24	34.5
Merula flavirostris	West coast Mexico	ad. ♂	4	125	99.7	21	32.6
Merula flavirostris	do	ad. ♀	5	124.4	98	24	32.4

BIRDS ERRONEOUSLY ATTRIBUTED TO THE TRES MARIAS.

Among the birds sent to the Smithsonian Institution from western Mexico by Mr. John Xantus are five species of humming birds named below which were not found on the Tres Marias either by Colonel Grayson or myself, and which are not known even from the adjacent parts of the mainland. These specimens are now in the National Museum, all labeled "Tres Marias, July, 1861." The improbability of their capture on the Tres Marias is very great, and the fact that species from such widely separated areas should be credited to these islands during a single month can be accounted for in only one way. Probably Mr. Xantus purchased these specimens from some one who misled him concerning their origin. That this could be done very easily I know from personal experience. Some years ago I purchased a small collection of birds from a San Francisco dealer, who claimed that they came from

La Paz, Lower California, but which proved to be made up of species found near Mazatlan, Sinaloa.

Thalurania luciæ Lawr.

Thalurania luciæ Lawr., Ann. Lyc. Nat. Hist., N. Y., VII, p. 2, 1867; Proc. Boston Soc. Nat. Hist., XIV, p. 284, 1871; Mem. Boston Soc. Nat. Hist., II, p. 291, 1874.

Described as new from the specimen sent in by Xantus, but proved to be *Thalurania glaucopis*, a resident of southeastern Brazil.

Florisuga mellivora (Linn.).

Lawr., Proc. Boston Soc. Nat. Hist., XIV, p. 284, 1871; Mem. Boston Soc. Nat. Hist., II, p. 291, 1874.

A well-known species of the humid tropics from southern Mexico to South America. There is no authentic record for it in western Mexico, and it is safe to say it has not been taken on the Tres Marias.

Uranomitra guatemalensis (Gould).

Lawr., Proc. Boston Soc. Nat. Hist., XIV, p. 284, 1871; Mem. Boston Soc. Nat. Hist., II, p. 292, 1874.

A species which ranges from Guatemala and British Honduras southward. There is no authentic Mexican record.

Petasophora thalassina (Swainson).

Lawr., Proc. Boston Soc. Nat. Hist., XIV, p. 284, 1871; Mem. Boston Soc. Nat. Hist., II, p. 292, 1874.

This humming bird ranges from the highlands about the Valley of Mexico southward into Central America, but there appears to be no authentic record for western Mexico.

Chlorostilbon insularis Lawr.

Chlorostilbon insularis Lawr., Ann. Lyc. Nat. Hist. N. Y., VII, p. 457, 1867; Proc. Boston Soc. Nat. Hist., XIV, p. 284, 1871; Mem. Boston Soc. Nat. Hist., II, p. 292, 1874.

This bird was described by Mr. Lawrence from a Xantus specimen, but proved to be *Chlorostilbon pucherani* of southeastern Brazil.

Merula grayi Lawr.

Merula grayi Lawr., Proc. Boston Soc. Nat. Hist., XIV, p. 276, 1871; Mem. Boston Soc. Nat. Hist., II, p. 266, 1874.

Grayson's notes on *Merula grayi* on the Tres Marias refer to pale specimens of *M. graysoni*, and his record of *M. grayi* at the city of Tepic, on the adjacent mainland, refers to *M. tristis*. *Merula tristis* is a common and widely spread species in suitable localities in western Mexico and is the only *Merula* sent in by Grayson from the city of Tepic.

Merula grayi, on the contrary, does not appear to occur anywhere in western Mexico north of the Isthmus of Tehuantepec, for no specimens were taken by Grayson nor, during our own work at many localities between the Isthmus and Mazatlan, has a single individual been noted, and there appears to be no authentic record of its occurrence there. This thrush is a species of the humid tropics, ranging along both coasts of Central America north to the Isthmus of Tehuantepec, and thence northward its range is limited to the humid region of the Gulf coast and adjacent mountain slopes of eastern Mexico.

REPTILES OF THE TRES MARIAS AND ISABEL ISLANDS.

By Leonhard Stejneger,

Curator, Division of Reptiles and Batrachians, U. S. National Museum.

The present paper is based upon the collection made on the Tres Marias and Isabel Islands in April and May, 1897, by E. W. Nelson and E. A. Goldman.

The surprising fact that the two expeditions which have collected systematically in the Tres Marias brought home the same number of species, Forrer only collecting one snake, *Diplotropis diplotropis*, which Nelson did not collect, and Nelson also collecting only one snake which Forrer did not obtain, viz, *Boa imperator*, seems to indicate that not many more species than the 16 here enumerated are to be found in these islands.

It will thus be seen that the reptile fauna is an exceedingly poor one and very disappointing in several respects. Thus most of the species are common on the opposite mainland and generally distributed over tropical Mexico and Central America. Then, again, it seems as if the species are practically identical on all the islands of the group. This would indicate a comparatively recent severance of the islands from each other as well as from the opposite mainland of Mexico.

It is worthy of note, perhaps, that there is absolutely no indication of relation to the Cape Saint Lucas fauna of Lower California. The only species occurring in both places is *Phyllodactylus tuberculosus*, a gecko of wide distribution, the presence of which is of absolutely no moment in determining zoogeographical relations.

The only species which seems to be peculiar to the islands is *Cnemidophorus mariarum*. As will be explained more fully under the head of this species, I have never seen a specimen from the mainland, and those which have been recorded from there I regard as wrongly identified. However, the herpetology of the regions in question is too little explored in detail to incline one to be dogmatic on a point like this, but I may call attention to the fact that the swift which occurs on the little Isabel Island, about halfway between the Tres Marias and the mainland, is most certainly the same form which inhabits the latter, viz, *Cnemidophorus gularis mexicanus*, and not *C. mariarum*, to which it bears only a superficial resemblance. The species collected on Isabel Island are referred to in the following paper without any number preceding the specific names. Mr. Nelson has contributed field notes on some of the species, and these notes are given in brackets with his initials at the end of the paragraph on the species to which they refer.

TESTUDINATA.

[The tortoise-shell turtle frequents the sea about the Tres Marias, approaching the shores to mate and deposit eggs in May and June each year. At the same time the large green sea turtle abounds along these shores, where they congregate for the same purpose.—E. W. N.]

Kinosternon integrum Leconte.

I have no hesitation in endorsing Boulenger's view (Cat. Chel. Brit. Mus., p. 42) that the Tres Marias mud turtles are *K. integrum* and not *K. hirtipes*, as held by Günther (Biol. Centr. Am., Rept., p. 15, pls. xii–xiv). They have the broader bridge and broader plastron of the former and agree with undoubted specimens from the mainland. The island specimens, of which there are four adults and one young, do not differ from those from Colima, Guañajuato, Cuernavaca (Morelos), Acaponeta (Tepic), Guadalajara (Jalisco), Presidio, and Mazatlan (Sinaloa), from all of which localities I have examined specimens. *K. hirtipes* I believe to be confined to the eastern side of Mexico.

List of specimens of Kinosternon integrum.

U. S. National Museum number.	Collectors' number.	Locality.	Date.
24696	712	Maria Madre Island	May 15, 1897
24697	713	..... do	May 15, 1897
24698	714	..... do	May 15, 1897
24699	715	..... do	May 15, 1897
24610	716	..... do	May 15, 1897

LORICATA.

Crocodylus americanus Laur.

No specimens were secured, but Mr. Nelson assures me that the crocodile occurs on Maria Magdalena Island. There can be but little doubt that it is the present species which is distributed all along the coast of Central America, Mexico, the West Indies, and southern Florida.

[The unmistakable furrow in the mud where a crocodile had hauled up on the border of a brackish lagoon on the eastern side of Maria Magdalena, the sight of a small head in the water, and the testimony of the people on Maria Madre established the fact of their occurrence. They appeared to be limited to Maria Magdalena.—E. W. N.]

SQUAMATA.

SAURI.

Phyllodactylus tuberculosus Wiegm.

This species is distributed over Mexico and Central America, and has also been collected in the Cape Saint Lucas region of Lower California, the specimens from the latter locality having been described by Cope as *Phyllodactylus xanti.*

List of specimens of Phyllodactylus tuberculosus.

U. S. National Museum number.	Collectors' number.	Locality.	Date.
24611	669	Maria Madre Island	May 21, 1897
24612	¹686	.....do	May 28, 1897
24613	700	Maria Cleofa Island	May 30, 1897

¹ No. 686 was taken in an old house.

Anolis nebulosus Wiegm.

All the specimens from the three islands are normally colored and alike, except No. 692, which has a wide whitish dorsal band originating on the occiput and extending down the upper surface of the tail. It is edged with dusky, and a narrow broken line of the same dusky color in the white band near the edge on each side extends from neck to rump. This specimen is small and without gular pouch; but No. 691, from the same island, which equals it in these respects, is colored like the larger specimens. Both specimens appear to be females, having no enlarged postanal scales.

This species is widely distributed over Mexico, and has been collected in the Tres Marias Islands not only by Forrer but also by Capt. William Lund, specimens from the latter being in the museum of the California Academy of Sciences in San Francisco (Van Denburgh, Proc. Phila. Acad., 1897, p. 460).

List of specimens of Anolis nebulosus.

U. S. National Museum number.	Collectors' number.	Locality.	Date.
24614	636	Maria Madre Island	May 3, 1897
24615	641	.....do	May 4, 1897
24616	¹683	Maria Magdalena Island	May 28, 1897
24617	¹684	.....do	May 28, 1897
24618	¹685	.....do	May 28, 1897
24619	688	.....do	May 28, 1897
24620	690	Maria Cleofa Island	May 29, 1897
24621	691	.....do	May 29, 1897
24622	692	.....do	May 29, 1897

¹ Nos. 683–685 were found living in an old house.

Ctenosaura teres (Harlan). Black Iguana.

The material at hand is very unsatisfactory inasmuch as all the full-grown specimens are of the same sex and in rather poor state of preservation, while the younger specimens afford no characters for satisfactorily separating the various forms which naturally group themselves around *Ctenosaura teres*. They are therefore left under that general name for the present, the writer hoping some day to be able to review the whole genus. The chief difficulty now lies in the lack of typical specimens of *C. teres* from Tampico and from the eastern coast of Mexico generally, and until a series of full-grown specimens of both sexes is obtained from that region it will be futile to attempt to straighten out the nomenclature of these lizards. As far as I can make out from my defective material the Tres Marias and Isabel specimens differ sufficiently from specimens from Colima and Tehuantepec to warrant their subspecific recognition, but whether identical with the Mazatlan form or not I am not able to say. There are certainly several pretty well defined races of this species; but more adult specimens and a direct comparison with the types of many of the old names in various foreign museums will be necessary before the intricate questions involved can be settled.

[The females were burrowing in the gravel in dry washes and flats on the islands the last half of May. The burrows were from 2 to 3 or 4 feet deep, and after the eggs had been deposited at the lower end, the female scraped in loose gravel until the hole was filled, and frequently raised a little mound over the entrance.—E. W. N.]

U. S. National Museum number.	Collectors' number.	Locality.	Date.
24623	655	Maria Madre Island	May 14, 1897
24624	656	..... do	May 14, 1897
24625	659	..... do	May 15, 1897
24626	660	..... do	May 15, 1897
24627	662	..... do	May 15, 1897
24628	(bis) 662	..... do	May 17, 1897
24629	676	..... do	May 24, 1897
24630	683	Maria Cleofa Island	May 29, 1897
24631	630	Isabel Island	Apr. 23, 1897
24632	631	..... do	Apr. 23, 1897
24633	632	..... do	Apr. 23, 1897

Uta lateralis Boulenger.

Mr. Nelson remarks that this species lives on stones and driftwood near the border of the woods along the sea beaches.

Uta lateralis was based by Boulenger in 1883 upon specimens from the Tres Marias and from Presidio, near Mazatlan, collected by Forrer, and specimens from both localities are designated as 'types' in the 'Catalogue of Lizards in the British Museum.'

U. S. National Museum number.	Collectors' number.	Locality.	Date.
24634	635	Maria Madre Island	May 3, 1897
24635	642	...do	May 4, 1897
24636	643	...do	May 7, 1897
24637	653	...do	May 13, 1897
24638	670	...do	May 21, 1897
24639	671	...do	May 21, 1897
24640	672	...do	May 21, 1897
24641	673	...do	May 21, 1897
24642	674	...do	May 21, 1897
24643	675	...do	May 21, 1897
24644	678	...do	May 25, 1897
24645	679	...do	May 25, 1897

Sceloporus boulengeri Stejneger.

N. Am. Fauna No. 7, 1893, p. 180, pl. I, figs. 5a–c.

This species appears to be smaller than *S. clarkii*, of which it is the southern representative. A full-grown male (No. 634c) measures only 72^{mm} from snout to vent.

Van Denburgh's belief that *S. boulengeri* "is the same form as Cope's *S. oligoporus*" (Proc. Phila. Acad., 1897, p. 463) is not well founded. The latter is easily distinguished by having only 2 to 3 femoral pores, besides other differences. It is probably identical with *S. horridus*.

U. S. National Museum number.	Collectors' number.	Locality.	Sex.	Number of pores.	Date.
24646	634	Isabel Island	♂ ad...	8	Apr. 23, 1897
24647	634 a	...do	♀ juv...	9	Apr. 23, 1897
24648	634 b	...do	♂ adol..	7	Apr. 23, 1897
24649	634 c	...do	♀ ad...	9	Apr. 23, 1897
24650	634 d	...do	♀	9	Apr. 23, 1897
24651	634 e	...do	♂ ad...	9	Apr. 23, 1897

Cnemidophorus mariarum Günther.

Cnemidophorus mariarum Günther Biol. Cent.-Am., Rept. p. 28, pl. XX, April, 1885; Boulenger, Cat. Lizards, Brit. Mus., p. 368, 1885.

The swifts from the Tres Marias are essentially alike. Those from Maria Madre are the largest and possibly also most distinctly marked; those from the small detached rock off the west side of Maria Cleofa as well as the one from the main island of that name are somewhat smaller. According to Mr. Nelson's observation those from the detached islet, which is a bare rock, the nesting place of numerous sea birds, appeared to him paler when alive than those on the other islands, but now, in alcohol, the difference, if any, is very slight.

This species, which was originally described by Günther from specimens collected by Forrer on the Tres Marias seems to be confined to this group of islands. If so, it is the only species of reptile hitherto

collected which is peculiar to these islands. The species has been
recorded from the mainland (by Van Denburgh, Proc. Phila. Acad., 1897,
p. 463, who identifies "a large number of lizards from Mazatlan, San
Blas, and Tepic" with Günther's species), but I am satisfied that these
records are based upon specimens of *C. gularis mexicanus* (Peters)
which superficially very much resemble the island species. The mis-
identification is probably due to the fact that Cope, in his monograph
of the genus, overlooked the different keeling of the caudal scales
which is the essential character of this species.

List of specimens of Cnemidophorus mariarum.

U. S. National Museum number.	Collectors' number.	Locality.	Date.
24652	637	Maria Madre Island	May 3, 1897
24653	638	....do	May 3, 1897
24654	639	....do	May 4, 1897
24655	640	....do	May 4, 1897
24656	644	....do	May 7, 1897
24657	645	....do	May 7, 1897
24658	646	....do	May 7, 1897
24659	647	....do	May 7, 1897
24660	687	Maria Magdalena Island	May 28, 1897
24661	701	Maria Cleofa Island (outlying rock)	May 30, 1897
24662	702	....do	May 30, 1897
24663	703	....do	May 30, 1897
24664	704	....do	May 30, 1897
24665	705	....do	May 30, 1897
24666	706	Maria Cleofa Island (main island)	May 31, 1897

Cnemidophorus gularis mexicanus (Peters).

The Isabel Island swifts are identical with the mainland form, two
specimens of which were brought from San Blas. They are quite distinct from the species on the Tres Marias, which is well characterized
by the smaller femorals and the parallel caudals. It is strange that
Cope, having had the latter character clearly pointed out by Boulenger,
should have referred *C. mariarum* to *C. gularis* as a subspecies.

List of specimens of Cnemidophorus gularis mexicanus.

U. S. National Museum number.	Collectors' number.	Locality.	Date.
24667	633	Isabel Island	April 23, 1897
24668	633a	....do	April 23, 1897
24669	633b	....do	April 23, 1897
24670	633c	....do	April 23, 1897
24671	633d	....do	April 23, 1897

SERPENTES.

Boa imperator Daudin.

This is the first record of this species from the Tres Marias. The species is generally distributed through southern Mexico and Central America.

Scale rows 73.

List of specimens of Boa imperator.

U. S. National Museum number.	Collectors' number.	Locality.	Date.
24672	648	Maria Madre Island	May 12, 1897

Oxybelis acuminatus (Wied).

A common species occurring all through tropical America from Guaymas, Mexico, south.

List of specimens of Oxybelis acuminatus.

U. S. National Museum number.	Collectors' number.	Locality.	Date.
24673	677	Maria Madre Island	May 25, 1897

Diplotropis diplotropis (Günther).

This species seems to be confined to western Mexico. It was not collected by Mr. Nelson, but there are two specimens in the British Museum collected by Forrer on the Tres Marias (*Leptophis diplotropis* Boulenger, Cat. Snakes Brit. Mus., II, p. 110).

Drymobius boddaerti (Seetzen).

A common species distributed over tropical America.

In No. 681 the fourth labials on both sides are divided horizontally, so as to suggest a subpreocular. This is an adult male, and is uniformly colored above, without any markings. The adolescent specimens are uniform above, with a few scales tipped with black; the anterior part of the underside has square blackish spots. The two young ones have above brown, dark-edged, squarish spots, separated by narrow light-colored interspaces. They are marked underneath like the adolescent specimens.

No. 681, male ad.—Scale rows, 17; ventrals, 183; anal, ½; caudals, $\frac{111}{111}$; supralabials, 9.

List of specimens of Drymobius boddaerti.

U. S. National Museum number.	Collectors' number.	Locality.	Date.
24674	652 juv.	Maria Madre Island	May 12, 1897
24675	654 ad.	.....do	May 13, 1897
24676	658 ad.	.....do	May 14, 1897
24677	661 ad.	.....do	May 15, 1897
24678	663 juv.	.....do	May 18, 1897
24679	681 ad.	Maria Magdalena Island	May 27, 1897

Bascanion lineatum Bocourt.

This species is apparently confined to western Mexico.

List of specimens of Bascanion lineatum.

U. S. National Museum number.	Collectors' number.	Locality.	Date.
24680	650	Maria Madre Island	May 12, 1897
24681	651	.....do	May 12, 1897
24682	660	.....do	May 16, 1897

Drymarchon corais melanurus (Dum. & Bibr.)

Scale rows, 19; ventrals, 205; anal, 1; caudals, $\frac{53}{53}$, supralabials, 8. Adult male with the characteristic coloring of this subspecies, which seems to be confined to Mexico and Central America.

List of specimens of Drymarchon corais melanurus.

U. S. National Museum number.	Collectors' number.	Locality.	Date.
24683	664	Maria Madre Island	May 18, 1897

Lampropeltis micropholis oligozona (Bocourt).

Scale rows, 23; ventrals, 230; anal, 1; caudals, $\frac{5}{11}$; temporals, $2 + 3$. Adult male. Thirteen annuli on body, separated by wide, red interspaces, without black spots, both on back and belly; all the annuli complete, including that on neck and throat, which does not touch the parietals; snout white, with black on rostral and anterior nasal. From Boulenger's account it appears that Forrer's specimens from the Tres Marias are identical. (Cat. Snakes Brit. Mus., II, p. 204.)

Distributed over Mexico and Central America.

List of specimens of Lampropeltis micropholis oligozona.

U. S. National Museum number.	Collectors' number.	Locality.	Date.
24684	663	Maria Madre Island	May 16, 1897

Agkistrodon bilineatus (Günther).

Scale rows, 23; ventrals, 138; anal, 1; caudals, 21 + $\frac{2}{8}$. Adult male.
Southern Mexico and Central America to Nicaragua.

List of specimens of Agkistrodon bilineatus.

U. S. National Museum number.	Collectors' number.	Locality.	Date.
24685	707	Maria Madre Island	May 15, 1897

Crotalus sp. ?

No rattlesnake was collected on the Tres Marias by Forrer, nor by Nelson, but the latter informs me that he was told of the occurrence of a rattler on Maria Magdalena Island.

NOTES ON THE CRUSTACEA OF THE TRES MARIAS ISLANDS.

By MARY J. RATHBUN,

Second Assistant Curator, Division of Marine Invertebrates, U. S. National Museum.

Of the four species of crustacea taken by E. W. Nelson and E. A. Goldman on the Tres Marias Islands in May, 1897, two are identical with forms inhabiting Lower California, one is found in all the warm countries of the world, while the fourth, a fresh-water shrimp, is distributed throughout tropical America.

Gecarcinus digueti Bouvier.

Gecarcinus digueti Bouvier, Bull. Mus. Hist. Nat., Paris, I, 8, 1895.

Maria Cleofa Island. May 30. One large male (Collectors' No. 717).

The type and only specimen hitherto collected is from Lower California, and is in the Paris Museum. This species differs from others found on the Pacific coast in its wider carapace, narrower front, longer legs, and in the form of the abdomen of the male.

Measurements.

Specimen.	Length.	Width.	Exorbital width.	Inferior width of front.	Length of merus of second ambulatory leg.	Width of same.	Length of carpus.	Width of same.	Length of propodus.	Width of same.	Length of dactylus.	Width of same.
Type, ♂, Lower California	46.3	69	25	9	33	9.7	26	8	17	7.3	24.2	3.7
♂, Maria Cleofa Island	76	104	37.5	13	46.3	13.4	22.5	11.5	21.5	10	33.5	5

The measurements of the legs are exclusive of the large spines, and the length given is that of the anterior or superior margin. The penultimate segment of the abdomen of the male is very wide. Length and distal width, 12 mm.; proximal width, 21.5.

Mr. Nelson says of these crabs:

On the Tres Marias we found them only on Maria Cleofa, where they were very numerous above high-water mark on the sandy beaches of the low eastern part of the island. They were also living very abundantly in burrows in the soft soil almost everywhere on the slopes of Isabel Island. They are nocturnal in habits, and caused

73

some annoyance by walking over us at night while we were camped in their haunts. They began to come out of their burrows as soon as it became twilight in the evening. In both localities most of their burrows were found among the scrubby bushes. On Isabel Island they were often seen during the day sitting in the burrows a foot or so from the entrance, but scuttled back to a safe depth when I approached.

Ocypode[1] occidentalis Stimpson.

   Ocypoda occidentalis Stimpson, Ann. Lyc. Nat. Hist. N. Y., VII, 229, 1860.

   Maria Magdalena Island. May 28. One female (No. 689).
   Maria Cleofa Island. May 30. One male (No. 699).

This much neglected species is distinct, it seems to me, from *O. kuhlii* de Haan, of which Miers made it a variety. According to the description of *O. kuhlii* given by de Man (Notes Leyden Mus., III, 250, 1881), who had the type before him, *O. occidentalis* differs from it in having a narrower carapace, in the outer orbital angle directed inward and not outward, in the shorter hand, the length of the upper margin of the palm being less than the width, and in having from 18 to 21 tubercles in the stridulating ridge (de Man gives 8 or 10 for *kuhlii*, while Miers figures 17). The form of the abdomen of the male furnishes excellent characters for the determination of the species of *Ocypode*. In *O. occidentalis* the penultimate segment is much wider at its middle than at its proximal end.

It is singular that this species is not mentioned in the revisions of the genus by Kingsley, 1880, or by Ortmann, 1897.

Dimensions of a type specimen, U. S. National Museum.—Male: Length, 40.5 mm.; epibranchial width, 48; exorbital width, 41; length of superior margin of palm, 22.8; entire length of propodus, 43.5; greatest width, 24.

Range.—Type locality, Cape St. Lucas. Also taken at Turtle Bay and San Jose del Cabo, Lower California, by Mr. A. W. Anthony, in 1896 and 1897.

Grapsus grapsus (Linnæus).

"This crab was very abundant on the rocks along the water's edge on the Tres Marias as well as on Isabel Island." (Nelson.)

The species is distributed throughout the tropics.

Bithynis jamaicensis (Herbst).

   Maria Magdalena Island. May 27. One adult, 7 young (No. 709).
   Maria Cleofa Island. May 30. One adult, 3 young (No. 710).

"These shrimps were very numerous in a small stream among the hills in the interior of Maria Magdalena, and were also numerous in streams flowing through the hilly parts of the adjacent mainland." (Nelson.)

The species is found on the Pacific slope of the continent from Lower California to Ecuador, and on the Atlantic slope from Texas to Rio de Janeiro. The following localities, not before recorded, are represented by specimens in the U. S. National Museum: On the Pacific

[1] *Ocypode*, not *Ocypoda*, Fabricius, Entom. Sys., Suppl., 312 and 347, 1798; also Entom. Sys., emend. et auct., IV, index, 115, 1796.

coast, La Paz, Lower California; Rio Presidio, Sinaloa; Rio de Alica, Tepic; Barranca Ibarra, Rio Santiago, Jalisco, and Rio Armeria, Colima, Mexico; Rio de los Platanales and Quebrada Chavarria Golfito (both tributary to the Gulf of Dulce), Costa Rica; River David, Chiriqui, United States of Colombia, 4,000 feet elevation; Guayaquil, Ecuador. On the Atlantic coast, San Antonio, Tex.; Las Moras Creek, Kinney County, Tex.; Brownsville, near mouth of Rio Grande, Tex.: Amixtlan, and Zacatlan, Puebla, Mexico; Escondido River, 50 miles from Bluefields, Nicaragua; Port Castries, St. Lucia, West Indies.

The west African form, *B. vollenhovenii* (Herklots) is no more than a subspecies of *B. jamaicensis*. It differs only in the slenderer second pair of feet, the carpal and meral joints of which are subequal. The relative lengths of the rostrum and the antennal scales and peduncles agree with those in some specimens of *jamaicensis*. The two forms are considered identical by Dr. Ortmann.

According to Dr Edward Palmer, *B. jamaicensis* is much eaten at Colima, and is offered in the market there as a choice article of food, especially on Fridays and Sundays.

PLANTS OF THE TRES MARIAS ISLANDS.

By J. N. Rose,

Assistant Curator, Division of Plants, U. S. National Museum.[1]

The Tres Marias, lying about 65 miles off the west coast of Mexico in about 22° north latitude, are among the last of the west coast islands to be studied. All the others have yielded valuable botanical results, but almost nothing has been known of the flora of these islands except in a commercial way. Several botanical expeditions had been planned to explore the islands, but heretofore none had succeeded in reaching them. They are out of the line of traffic, although some of the smaller steamers stop now and then for fuel, and small boats occasionally ply between the islands and San Blas. They are usually visited during the dry season, as it is dangerous to attempt the passage during summer and autumn.

Mr. Nelson visited the islands at the very close of the dry season, when the vegetation is at its poorest, and this accounts for the small number of species collected. His collection contains 154 numbers (Nos. 4179 to 4333) and 136 species, mostly from Maria Madre, the largest of the islands, and only a few from Maria Magdalena and Maria Cleofa. In the subjoined list the plants are from Maria Madre unless otherwise stated.

There are no cultivated plants on the islands, except one or two grasses. *Pithecolobium dulce*, perhaps introduced, is common and much prized for its delicious fruit. The exportation of Spanish cedar (*Cedrela* sp.) has long been the chief source of income for the islands, but the available supply of this timber is now nearly exhausted. The flora is purely tropical and does not differ essentially from that of the adjacent mainland. Many of the species have not been reported from the mainland opposite, but this is doubtless because the flora is not well known, since these species have been collected either farther north or south. One hundred and twelve species are named below, of which 11 are new. Many of them have a wide distribution in tropical America; all but 6, except the new species, have heretofore been reported from Mexico; 24 range northward into the United States; 64 extend into Central America; 61 into South America; 44 into the West Indies, and 21 are found in the Old World.

[1] Published by permission of the Secretary of the Smithsonian Institution.

The following report must be regarded as a preliminary one. The specimens upon which it is based are simply those in fruit or flower at the close of the dry season, a considerable number of which have not been determined specifically and a few not even generically. As will be seen from the list below, mostly trees and shrubs were collected, while the herbs, which spring up in great variety during the rainy season, are scarcely represented.

The Gamopetalæ and Apetalæ have been named by Mr. J. M. Greenman, Gramineæ by Prof. F. Lamson-Scribner, and Filices by George E. Davenport.

The following new species and varieties are based on this collection:

Ægiphila pacifica Greenman.	*Euphorbia subcarulea tresmariæ* Millsp.
Beloperone nelsoni Greenman.	*Gilibertia insularis* Rose.
Buxus pubescens Greenman.	*Pilocarpus insularis* Rose.
Cordia *insularis* Greenman.	*Ternstrœmia maltbya* Rose.
Erythrina *lanata* Rose.	*Zanthoxylum insularis* Rose.
Euphorbia nelsoni Millsp ngh.	*Zanthoxylum nelsoni* Rose.

ANNOTATED LIST OF SPECIES.

Cissampelos pareira L.

Common in Mexico and other tropical countries. May 3 to 25 (Nos. 4233 and 4262).

Argemone ochroleuca Sweet.

Widely distributed throughout Mexico. Maria Magdalena Island, May 26 to 28, 1897 (No. 4318).

Capparis cynophallophora L.

Found along the coast of Mexico, South America, and the West Indies. May 3 to 25 (No. 4302).

Capparis breynia L.

Common in Mexico, South America, and the West Indies. May 3 to 25 (No. 4219).

Cratæva tapia L. ?

Perhaps this is the species which has been reported from Acapulco and Mazatlan. May 3 to 25 (No. 4274.)

Ternstrœmia maltbya Rose, sp. nov.

Tree 3 to 9 meters high; leaves obovate, entire, obtuse, glabrous, thickish, not black-punctate beneath, 5 to 10 cm. long; flowers solitary; peduncles 2.5 to 3.5 cm. long becoming curved, bracteate a short distance below the calyx; sepals 5, orbicular, 8 to 10 mm. in diameter; petals united at base, acute; stamens numerous; fruit (immature) ovate, 20 mm. long, two-celled; seeds red.

This species is in all probability Seeman's No. 2148, collected on the road from Mazatlan to Durango and enumerated in the Biologia Centrali-Americana without specific name.

Collected on Maria Madre Island, May, 1897, by T. S. Maltby (No. 105) and E. W. Nelson (No. 4242); by J. N. Rose near Colomo, Sinaloa, July, 1897 (No. 1675).

Wissadula hirsutiflora (Presl) Rose.

The type of this species came from Acapulco. It is probably common on the west coast, although its distribution and specific limits are not well known. May 3 to 25 (No. 4250).

Abutilon reventum Watson.

This species extends as far north as Arizona. May 3 to 25 (No. 4203).

Hibiscus tiliaceus L.

A common tree in most tropical countries. Maria Magdalena Island, May 26 to 28 (No. 4328a).

Melochia tomentosa L.

Common throughout tropical America. May 3 to 25 (No. 4205).

Guazuma ulmifolia Lam.

Common throughout tropical America. Maria Magdalena Island, May 26 to 28 (No. 4325).

Heteropterys floribunda H. B. K.

Common in Mexico and Central America.
Maria Magdalena Island, May 26 to 28 (No. 4323).

Guaiacum coulteri ? Gray.

Seemingly common on the west coast of Mexico. Island specimens do not correspond with the form found on the mainland and may represent an undescribed species. May 3 to 25 (No. 4180).

Zanthoxylum insularis Rose, sp. nov.

Tree 6 to 20 meters high, thornless; leaves oddly pinnate; leaflets 6 to 7 pairs, opposite, sessile, obovate to spatulate, obtuse or retuse, 2 to 3.5 cm. long, crenate, with large pellucid dots between the teeth and small scattered dots over the surface, glabrous; flowers unknown; fruit small, in a rather compact panicle; pedicels very short; stipe short and thick.

Collected by E. W. Nelson on Maria Madre Island. May 3 to 25, 1897 (No. 4278).

Zanthoxylum nelsoni Rose, sp. nov.

Tree 7.5 to 20 meters high, thornless(?); leaves oddly pinnate; leaflets about 6 pairs, distant, opposite, shortly petioled, 5 to 11 cm. long, rounded at base, long-acuminate, crenate, glabrous on both sides, thickly set with pellucid dots; inflorescence in small compact panicles; perianth complete; petals 4 (?); fruit large in dense head-like clusters, not stipitate.

A very peculiar species, unlike any Mexican one known to me. Collected by E. W. Nelson on Maria Madre Island. May 3 to 25, 1897 (No. 4279).

Pilocarpus insularis Rose, sp. nov.

Tree 3 to 6 meters high, glabrous throughout; leaflets usually in threes, some solitary or in rows, 5 to 7.5 cm. long, retuse at apex, cuneate at base, in the lateral ones more or less oblique; midvein prominent, lateral veins indistinct below, not very prominent above; racemes short and compact, 5 to 10 cm. long; fruiting pedicels horizontal, 16 mm. long; ovary deeply 4 or 5-lobed or parted, 1 to 4 lobes not maturing.

This species is near *P. longipes* of Mexico, but with somewhat different leaves, more compact inflorescence, etc. Collected by E. W. Nelson on Maria Madre Island. May 3 to 25, 1897 (No. 4307).

Amyris sp.

May 3 to 25, 1897 (No. 4237).

Picramnia sp.

A tree 4.5 to 7.5 meters high; flowers said to be greenish, but none with specimens. Much resembling the South American species *P. ciliata* Mast., but without flowers or fruit. Exact identification is doubtful. May 3 to 25 (No. 4276).

Ochna sp.

May 3 to 25 (No. 4238).

Bursera gummifera Jacq.

Common throughout tropical Mexico, Central America, the West Indies, and extending into Florida. May 3 to 25 (No. 4227).

Guarea sp.

May 3 to 25 (Nos. 4222 and 4230).

Trichilia spondioides Swartz.

Common in tropical America. May 3 to 25 (Nos. 4214 and 4309).

Ximenia americana L.

Common in most tropical countries. May 3 to 25 (No. 4224).

Schœpfia schreberi Gmel.

Seemingly rare, but has been collected in Mexico and South America. May 3 to 25, 1897 (No. 4271).

Hippocratea sp.

Maria Magdalena Island, May 26 to 28 (No. 4320). Maria Madre Island, May 3 to 25 (No. 4226).

Colubrina arborea Brandegee.

Reported from Lower California and the west coast of Mexico. May 3 to 25 (No. 4213).

Cissus sicyoides L.

A common species in tropical America. May 3 to 25 (No. 4198).

Serjania mexicana Willd.

A common species in tropical America. May 3 to 25 (No. 4231).

Paullinia sessiliflora Radl.

Heretofore only known from the type specimens collected by Dr. Edward Palmer in the State of Colima, Mexico. May 3 to 25 (No. 4210).

Urvillea ulmacea H. B. K.

Common in Mexico and northern South America. May 3 to 25 (No. 4277).

Cardiospermum corindum L.

A widely distributed species. Maria Magdalena Island, May 26 to 28 (No. 4328).

Crotalaria lupulina ? H. B. K.

Perhaps this species, which is common in Mexico, and extends into the United States. May 3 to 25 (No. 4248).

Tephrosia sp.

May 3 to 25 (No. 4193).

Desmodium sp.

May 3 to 25 (No. 4287).

Erythrina lanata Rose, sp. nov.

A small tree, 4.5 to 7.5 meters high, with a trunk 10 cm. in diameter; branches glabrous, bearing mostly single infrastipular spines; leaflets triangular, shortly acuminate, 5 to 10 cm. long, 5 to 7.5 cm. broad, glabrous or nearly so.

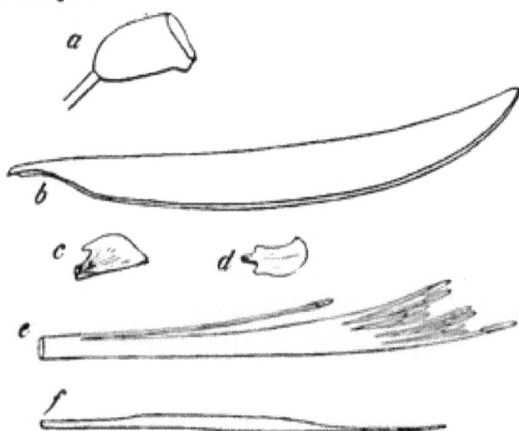

FIG. 1.—*Erythrina lanata; a, calyx; b, banner; c, keel; d, wing; e, stamens; f, ovary.*

Inflorescence unknown; calyx lanate becoming glabrate, tubular, 10 to 13 mm. long, truncate, one-toothed; banner 68 mm. long, folded, densely white-lanate, rounded at apex; wings (9 mm. long) and keel (10 mm. long) included within the calyx; ovary densely lanate; legume glabrous, 12.5 to 15 cm. long, strongly constricted between the seeds, long-stipitate, attenuate at tip; seeds small (for the genus), nearly orbicular, 6 to 8 mm. long, bright scarlet, with a dark spot at the micropyle.

13950—No. 14——6

The type of this species is Dr. Edward Palmer's No. 129, from Acapulco, Mexico, collected in 1894–95. To this species I would refer specimens collected by Frank Lamb near Villa Union, State of Sinaloa, January, 1893 (No. 428), and flowering specimens by W. C. Wright from the head of Mazatlan River, January, 1889 (No. 1292), and also those collected by J. N. Rose at Rosario. Sinaloa, July 10, 1897 (No. 1592), and July 22 (No. 1822). The latter two specimens are not in flower and their reference here is attended with some doubt. The seeds are larger and the pods less constricted between the seeds. Here also belongs E. W. Nelson's No. 4303 from the Tres Marias, collected May, 1897. I have tentatively referred to this species E. W. Nelson's No. 2699, taken at an altitude of 480 meters, near Santo Domingo, State of Oaxaca, June 18, 1895. It has similar pods, but is described as being but 6 to 12 cm. high and has more bluntish leaflets.

Dr. Palmer says this tree flowers in January, and is often used for hedge fences. It differs from all other Mexican species which I have seen in its white lanate banner. Its one-toothed calyx suggests E. rosea, but in the latter the calyx is described as obliquely truncate.

Phaseolus sp.

Maria Magdalena Island, May 26 to 28, 1897 (No. 4319).

Canavalia gladiata DC.

A species of wide distribution, perhaps throughout tropical America. May 3 to 25 (No. 4190).

Rhynchosia minima DC.

A common Mexican species extending into South America and the United States. May 3 to 25 (No. 4206).

Rhynchosia precatoria (?) (H. B. K.) DC.

This species has been reported from Acapulco and Panama. May 3 to 25 (No. 4179).

Lonchocarpus sp.

May 3 to 25 (No. 4310).

Ateleia (?) sp.

Without flowers or named specimens for comparison it is impossible to name this plant definitely. If it belongs to the genus Ateleia it is perhaps A. pterocarpa, the only species known from Mexico. A shrub or small tree 3.5 to 10.5 meters high. May 3 to 25 (No. 4186).

Cassia emarginata L.

Common in Mexico, South America, and the West Indies. May 3 to 25 (Nos. 4192 and 4297).

Cassia biflora L.

Common in tropical America. May 3 to 25 (Nos. 4194 and 4196).

Cassia atomaria L.

Common in Tropical Mexico and South America. Maria Magdalena Island, May 26 to 28 (No. 4321).

Bauhinia sp.

Apparently belonging to the genus *Bauhinia*, but very unlike any of the Mexican species with which I am familiar. A vine 6 to 9 meters long; only in fruit. May 3 to 25 (No. 4300).

Acacia sp.

This appears to be an undescribed species, of which I collected specimens on the mainland. May 3 to 25 (No. 4188).

Albizzia occidentalis Brandegee.

Probably the above species, which is found in Lower California and has been reported from western Mexico. May 3 to 25 (No. 4252).

Pithecolobium dulce Benth.

Common in tropical Mexico and South America. Often cultivated. May 3 to 25 (No. 4285).

Pithecolobium ligustrinum Klotzsch.

Common in tropical Mexico and northern South America. Maria Magdalena Island, May 26 to 28 (No. 4314).

Conocarpus erectus L.

Common throughout tropical America extending into Florida and reported from tropical Africa. May 3 to 25 (No. 4220).

Psidium sp.

Tree 6 to 9 meters high; flowers white; called 'palo prieto.' This species is not represented in the National Herbarium. May 3 to 25 (No. 4306).

Casearia corymbosa (?) H. B. K.

The Tres Marias specimens should probably be referred to this species although our herbarium material seems to represent more than one species. This form is common on the west coast of Mexico and Central America. May 3 to 25 (Nos. 4270 and 4308).

Casearia sylvestris Swartz.

Widely distributed throughout tropical Mexico, South America, and the West Indies. May 3 to 25 (No. 4241).

Casearia sp.

Maria Magdalena Island. May 26 to 28, 1897 (No. 4326).

Passiflora sp.

May 3 to 25 (No. 4249).

Opuntia sp.

May 3 to 25 (Nos. 4263 and 4286).

Gilibertia insularis Rose, sp. nov.

Tree 6 to 12 meters high; leaves 25 to 35 cm. long, including the slender petioles (7 to 18 cm. long), 9 to 20 cm. broad, entire or 3-lobed, oblong, rounded at base, rounded at apex or with a short acumination, glabrous, 3-nerved at base; fruiting inflorescence a short dense panicle;

rays 2 to 3 cm. long; pedicels 4 to 8 mm. long; fruit white, 6-lobed, 4 mm. high; styles short, connate to near the top.

Collected on Maria Madre Island May 3 to 25 (No. 4282).

Portlandia pterosperma Watson.

A species recently described by Dr. Watson, the type coming from near Guaymas, Sonora.   May 3 to 25 (No. 4211).

Eupatorium sp.

May 3 to 25, 1897 (No. 4225).

Eupatorium sp.

May 3 to 25, 1897 (No. 4244).

Eupatorium collinum DC.

Common in Mexico and Central America.   May 3 to 25, 1897 (No. 4199).

Mikania cordifolia Willd.

Reported from Central and South America.   May 3 to 25, 1897 (No. 4299).

Conyza lyrata H. B. K.

Reported from Mexico, Central and South America.   May 3 to 25 (Nos. 4290 and 4312).

Baccharis glutinosa Pers.

A common Mexican and Central American plant.   May 3 to 25, 1897 (No. 4291).

Pluchea odorata Cass.

Widely distributed in Mexico and South America.   May 3 to 25, 1897 (No. 4181).

Parthenium hysterophorus L.

Common in Mexico, South America, and in the southern United States.   May 3 to 25, 1897 (No. 4267).

Perityle microglossa Benth.

A common Mexican plant.   May 3 to 25, 1897 (No. 4266).

Porophyllum nummularium DC.

Restricted to Mexico.   May 3 to 25, 1897 (No. 4292).

Trixis frutescens P. Brown.

A common Mexican and Central American plant.   May 3 to 25, 1897 (Nos. 4191), and Maria Cleofa Island, May 30, 1897 (No. 4331).

Jacquinia macrocarpa Cav.

Species not represented in the National Herbarium, but reported from Mexico, and Central and South America.   May 3 to 25, 1897 (No. 4208).

Gonolobus sp.

Fruit only.   May 3 to 25, 1897 (No. 4313a).

Buddleia verticillata H. B. K.

A common Mexican species.   May 3 to 25, 1897 (No. 4183).

Cordia sonorae Rose.

A recently described species from Sonora. May 3 to 25, 1897 (No. 4207).

Cordia insularis Greenman.

Cordia insularis Greenman, Proc. Amer. Acad. 33: 483. 1898.

The original description is as follows: "Shrub 3 to 5.5 m. high; stems and branches glabrous, reddish brown, conspicuously dotted with numerous whitish lenticels; the extreme branchlets covered with hirsute pubescence; leaves scattered, elliptic-ovate or sometimes slightly obovate, 1.5 to 3 cm. long, 1 to 1.5 cm. broad, narrowed below into a short petiole, obtuse, the upper portion more or less deeply crenate-dentate, occasionally sharply toothed, entire toward the base, hispid above, spreading hirsute-pubescent beneath, especially on the midrib and veins; inflorescence capitulate; heads small (after the corolla has fallen, about 5 mm. in diameter); peduncles, during anthesis, 1 cm. or less in length, covered with a spreading hirsute pubescence; calyx 2 mm. long, 5-dentate; teeth short, acute; corolla 3 mm. long, nearly cylindrical, with short recurved lobes, externally glabrous, pubescent inside along the line of the filaments, stamens included; style a little exserted. Collected by E. W. Nelson on Maria Madre Island of the Tres Marias group of islands. May 3 to 25, 1897 (No. 4296)."

Tournefortia candida Walp.

Not previously in herbarium. May 3 to 25, 1897 (Nos. 4217 and 4229).

Tournefortia cymosa L.

I have only seen specimens from Guatemala. May 3 to 25, 1897 (No. 4189).

Tournefortia velutina H. B. K.

Reported from the west coast of Mexico and Guatemala. May 3 to 25, 1897 (No. 4209).

Heliotropium indicum L.

Common in Mexico and most tropical countries. May 3 to 25, 1897 (No. 4253).

Heliotropium curassavicum L.

Common in Mexico and South America as well as in the Old World. Reported in the United States as far north as Oregon and Virginia. May 3 to 25, 1897 (No. 4313).

Ipomoea bona-nox L.

A common tropical plant extending into Florida. May 3 to 25, 1897 (No. 4269).

Ipomoea peduncularis Bertol.

Common in Mexico and Central America. May 3 to 25, 1897 (No. 4235).

Jacquemontia violacea Choisy.

Reported from Mexico, Central and South America, and the West Indies. May 3 to 25, 1897 (No. 4251).

Solanum nigrum L.

A widely distributed species. May 3 to 25, 1897 (No. 4200).

Solanum lanceaefolium Jacq.

A common tropical plant. May 3 to 25, 1897 (No. 4240).

Solanum callicarpaefolium Kunth & Bouché.

Common in south Mexico and northern South America. Maria Magdalena Island, May 26 to 28, 1897 (No. 4322).

Solanum torvum Swartz.

Common in Mexico and Central America. May 3 to 25, 1897 (No. 4185).

Solanum verbascifolium L.

Only reported hitherto from one station in southern Mexico. May 3 to 25, 1897 (No. 4216).

Physalis pubescens L.

A common tropical plant. May 3 to 25, 1897 (No. 4255).

Bassovia donnell-smithii Coulter.

A recently described South American and Guatemalan species. May 3 to 25, 1897 (No. 4232).

Datura discolor Bernh.

Reported from Mexico and West Indies. May 3 to 25, 1897 (No. 4197).

Nicotiana trigonophylla Dun.

Common in Mexico. May 3 to 25, 1897 (No. 4212).

Russelia sarmentosa Jacq.

A common Mexican and Central American species. (May 3 to 25, 1897 (No. 4289).

Capraria biflora L.

A widely distributed plant, extending into Florida. May 3 to 25, 1897 (No. 4195).

Bignonia aequinoctialis L.   (*B. sarmentosa* Bertol.)

Recently collected at Acapulco by Dr. Edward Palmer. It is common in Central and South America. May 3 to 25, 1897 (No. 4301), and Maria Magdalena Island, May 26 to 28 (No. 4324).

Beloperone nelsoni Greenman.

Beloperone nelsoni Greenman, Proc. Amer. Acad. 33: 488.   1898.

"It is nearest *B. comosa* Nees, in DC. Prodr. 11: 416, but differs very markedly in the size of the flower and the character of the lower lip."— Greenman in litt. May 3 to 25, 1897 (No. 4246).

The original description is as follows: "Erect; stems branching, subterete, covered with a spreading or slightly reflexed grayish pubescence; leaves ovate-lanceolate or oblong-lanceolate, 5 to 10 cm. long, 2 to 4 cm. broad, obtuse at the apex, entire, narrowed below into a slender petiole, densely lineolate above, pubescent on either surface, especially on the veins, later becoming glabrous; petioles about 2 cm. in length; inflorescence terminating the stem and branches in rather close bracteate spikes; bracts oblong or obovate; bracteoles linear, nearly 1 cm. long, exceeding the calyx; calyx about 5 mm. long, deeply 5-parted; divisions nearly equal, lanceolate, acute, ciliate; corolla 2 to 2.5 cm. long; tube exceeding the limb; upper lip shortly 2-lobed, the lower more deeply 3-lobed, rather broad, somewhat plaited in the throat; capsule 10 to 12 mm. long, pubescent. Collected by E. W. Nelson on Maria Madre Island of the Tres Marias group of islands, 3–25 May, 1897 (No. 4246).

"A species closely resembling *B. comosa* Nees, but with a much shorter corolla, and broader lower lip. The leaves are also somewhat larger, longer-petioled, and much less pubescent. It may be that further material will prove this to be a variety of *B. comosa* Nees, but as the material at hand shows no sign of intergradation, it seems best for the present at least to regard Mr. Nelson's plant as a distinct species."

Lantana horrida H. B. K.

Reported from both northern and southern Mexico. May 3 to 25, 1897 (No. 4187).

Citharexylum affinis D. Don.

This is a rare Mexican species which has been "compared with the Prodromus specimen at Geneva by C. De Candolle"—J. M. G. May 3 to 25, 1897 (No. 4311).

Ægiphila pacifica Greenman.

Ægiphila pacifica Greenman, Proc. Amer. Acad. 33:185. 1898.

The original description is as follows: "Shrub 2.5 to 7 m. high; stems and branches terete, covered with a grayish brown bark and dotted here and there with lenticels, glabrous; branchlets terete, somewhat compressed at the nodes, fulvous-pubescent; leaves opposite, oblong-ovate, 5 to 15 cm. long, 3.5 to 7.5 cm. broad, more or less acuminate, entire, rounded or rather abruptly narrowed at the slightly unequal base, glabrous, or at least glabrate above, with scattered, tawny, subappressed hairs beneath, especially upon the midrib and veins; petioles less than 1 cm. in length; inflorescence terminating the stems and branches in rather close paniculate cymes; peduncles, pedicels, the subulate bracts and calyx covered by a fulvous subappressed pubescence; calyx about 4 mm. long, 4-lobed; lobes broader than long, submucronate, greenish; corolla tubular, 10 to 12 mm. long, glabrous; tube somewhat ampliated above; lobes oblong-elliptic, about 4 mm. long, obtuse; stamens equal or rarely unequal, exserted; filaments pubescent below, glabrous above; drupe yellow, obovoid, 8 to 10 mm. long, 6 to 8 mm. in diameter, one-half or more exserted from the persistent coriaceous subcrenately lobed, cup-shaped calyx.—Collected by E. W. Nelson on Maria Madre Island of the Tres Marias group of islands, 3–25 May, 1897, No. 4245 (in flower) and No. 4254 (in fruit)."

Hyptis albida H. B. K.

Several times reported from Mexico. May 3 to 25, 1897 (No. 4223).

Salvia aliena Greene.

A Mexican species. May 3 to 25, 1897 (No. 4247).

Stachys coccinea Jacq.

Common in Mexico and Central America, extending into Texas and Arizona. May 3 to 25, 1897 (No. 4265).

Iresine interrupta Benth.

Reported from western and central Mexico. May 3 to 25, 1897 (No. 4234).

Phytolacca octandra L.

May 3 to 25, 1897 (No. 4293).

Stegnosperma halimifolia Benth.

Common along the west coast of Mexico. May 3 to 25, 1897 (No. 4184).

Batis maritima L.

Extending from Florida and California to Brazil and the West Indies and also reported from the Sandwich Islands. Magdalena Island, May 26 to 28, 1897 (No. 4327).

Coccoloba leptostachya Benth.

This species has not been heretofore found in Mexico, but has been reported from Central America and South America. Maria Magdalena Island, May 26 to 28, 1897 (No. 4315).

Antigonon leptopus Hook. & Arn.

A very common vine on the west coast of Mexico. May 3 to 25, 1897 (No. 4201).

Aristolochia pardina Duch.

A little-known plant collected at Colima many years ago by Ghiesbrecht, and recently at the same place by Dr. Edward Palmer. May 3 to 25, 1897 (No. 4304).

Piper aduncum L.

Reported from Mexico, Central and South America, and the West Indies. May 3 to 25, 1897 (No. 4283).

Euphorbia sp.

May 3 to 25, 1897 (No. 4268).

Euphorbia subcaerulea tresmariae Millspaugh, var. nov.

"In the characters present in the specimens collected, this agrees well with *E. subcaerulea* Rob. and Greenm. (Pringle No. 6265, Oaxaca), except in the hairy involucre more regularly toothed involucral lobes, and in having the styles bifurcate, to the middle only, and flat-spreading with no tendency to reflexion or peltation as in the other species. The fruits may prove this to be a distinct species. May 3 to 25, 1897 (Nos. 4298 and 4202)."—Millspaugh MSS.

Euphorbia sp.

Specimens are indeterminable from lack of characters. May 3 to 25, 1897 (No. 4215).

Euphorbia nelsoni Millspaugh.

Euphorbia nelsoni Millspaugh, Bot. Gaz. 26:268. 1898.

May 3 to 25, 1897 (No. 4294, not 4284, as published).

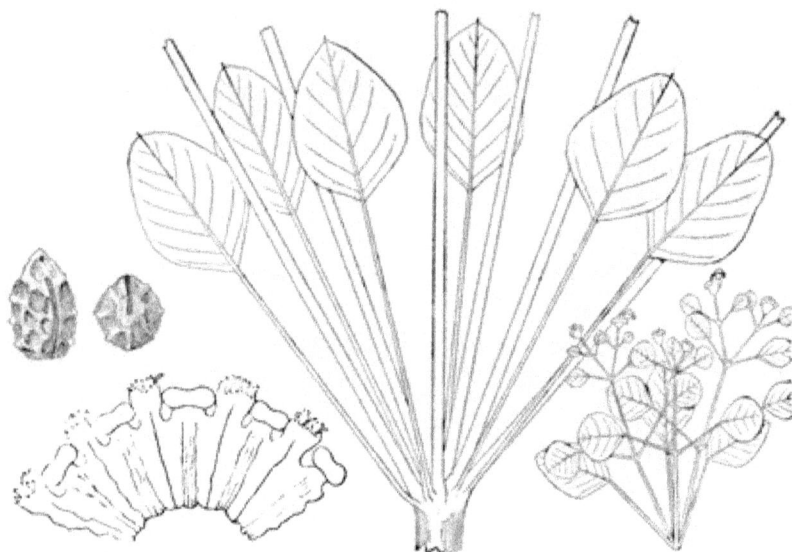

FIG. 2.—*Euphorbia nelsoni.*

The original description is as follows: " Fruticosa, glabra, longe et corymbosa ramosa, ramis teretis, internodiis longis, cortex maculatis, maculae oblongis roseus. Foliis inferioris fasciculatis, petioliis longis filamentosis, pagina tenuis ovato-cuneatis, obtusis, apiculatis, foliis floralibus oppositis, orbiculatis petiolis limbum aequantis. Involucriis terminalibus corymbosis, pedunculatis, campanulatis glabris, lobis latis truncatis irregulariter 6–8 fimbriatis, glandulis 5, transversis oblongis integris, appendicibus minutis vel nullus. Stylis longis revoluto-circinalis. Capsulae luridae profunde tri-sulcatae, semine sub-globosis pallide-fuscis, scrobiculatis, linea media nigra geminatis, rugae anasto-mosantis tuberculatis 2 mm. long, 1.9 mm. lat."

Several Euphorbias were collected on the islands in too imperfect condition to determine, and it has been thought advisable to reproduce the cut[1] of the present species for the purpose of assisting future study of the flora.

[1] Through the kindness of the editors of the Botanical Gazette I am permitted to use this illustration.

The main figure shows a cluster of leaves. To the right is a flower cluster and to the left a dissected flower with end and side views of the seed.

Garcia nutans Rohr.

Found in Mexico and South America. May 3 to 25, 1897 (No. 4228).

Croton ciliato-glandulosus Ort.

May 3 to 25, 1897 (No. 4218).

Acalypha sp.

May 3 to 25, 1897 (No. 4260).

Celtis monoica Hemsley.

May 3 to 25, 1897 (No. 4236).

Buxus pubescens Greenman.

Buxus pubescens Greenman, Proc. Amer. Acad. 33 : 481. 1898.

The original description is as follows: "Shrub or small tree, 4.5 to 8 m. high; stems and branches covered with a grayish bark; the branchlets and younger shoots provided with a soft, spreading pubescence; leaves opposite or occasionally subalternate, sessile or nearly so, rhombic-ovate to oblong-ovate, 2 to 5 cm. long, 1.5 to nearly 3 cm. broad, 3-nerved, obtuse or acutish, mucronate, cuneate at the base, entire, ciliate, soft-pubescent beneath, more sparingly pubescent and glabrate above, showing the reticulate venation on the upper surface; inflorescence of axillary short-pedunculate much contracted subracemose pubescent clusters; staminate flowers pedicellate; pedicels 3 mm. long, about twice exceeding the ovate acute bracts; calyx deeply 4-parted; divisions ovate, acute, 2 mm. long, the inner divisions slightly broader than the outer ones; the rudimentary pistil somewhat quatrefoil or X-shaped; fertile flowers about 5 mm. long, single, sessile, terminating the inflorescence; ovary glabrous; fruit not seen.—Collected on Maria Madre Island by E. W. Nelson, 3–25 May, 1897, No. 4221.

"A species apparently endemic in the Tres Marias Islands, and most nearly related to the West Indian *B. pulchella* Baill."

Ficus radulina Watson.

A recent species of Dr. Watson's from northern Mexico. May 3 to 25, 1897 (No. 4261).

Ficus fasciculata Watson.

Only known from western Mexico. May 3 to 25, 1897 (No. 4288).

Ficus sp.

May 3 to 25, 1897 (No. 4182).

Myriocarpa longipes Liebm.

Found in Mexico and Central America. May 3 to 25, 1897 (No. 4275).

Agave sp.

Six meters high, leaves 9 to 18 dm. long; marginal teeth small, distant; end spine short, stout, pungent; capsules oblong, large, 7 cm. long.

This species belongs to the subgenus *Eugare* and the *Rigidae* group of Mr. Baker's revision. It is near *A. vivipara*, and perhaps not distinct. Mr. Nelson's plant does not seem to differ from specimens collected by me on the mainland. May 3 to 25, 1897 (No. 4264).

Cyperus ligularis L.

Reported from Mexico, Central and South America, and West Indies, as well as Africa and Australia. Maria Cleofa Island, May 30, 1897 (No. 4330).

Cyperus incompletus Link.

Reported from Mexico and Brazil. May 3 to 25, 1897 (No. 4259).

Panicum brevifolium L.

May 3 to 25 (No. 4257).

Eleusine indica Gaertn.

May 3 to 25, 1897 (No. 4305).

Dactyloctenium aegyptiacum Willd.

May 3 to 25, 1897 (Nos. 4295 and 4256); Maria Magdalena Island, May 26 to 28 (No. 4317).

Arundo donax L.

Maria Cleofa Island, May 30 (No. 4332).

Zamia loddigesii (?) Miq.

Reported from Mexico. Maria Cleofa Island, May 30, 1897 (No. 4329).

Pteris longifolia L.

Maria Madre Island, May 3 to 25, 1897 (No. 4201).

Aspidium trifoliatum Swartz.

Maria Madre Island, May 3 to 25, 1897 (No. 4280).

Aspidium patens Swartz.

A widely distributed species. Maria Magdalena Island, May 26 and 28, 1897 (No. 4316).

Adiantum concinnum H. B. K.

Maria Madre Island, May 3 to 25, 1897 (No. 4273).

Adiantum tenerum Swartz.

Maria Madre Island, May 3 to 25, 1897 (No. 4281).

Gymnogramme calomelanos Kaulf.

A widely distributed species. Maria Cleofa Island, May 30, 1897 (No. 4333).

PARTIAL BIBLIOGRAPHY OF THE TRES MARIAS ISLANDS.

By E. W. NELSON.

1703. DAMPIER, WILLIAM. A New Voyage round the World, 5th ed., I, pp. 263–264. Notes the presence of seals about the Tres Marias. These notes are quoted by Allen and Alston.

1865. BAIRD, SPENCER F. <Review of American Birds, p. 232. Description of *Granatellus francescæ.*

1866. ALLEN, HARRISON. Notes on the *Vespertilionidæ* of Tropical America. <Proc. Acad. Nat. Sci. Phila. 1866, p. 285. Description of *Rhogeëssa parvula.*

1867. CASSIN, JOHN. A third study of the Icteridæ. <Proc. Acad. Nat. Sci. Phila. 1867, p. 48. Description of *Icterus graysoni.*

1867. LAWRENCE, GEORGE N. Descriptions of Six New Species of Birds of the Families *Hirundinidæ*, *Formicaridæ*, *Tyrannidæ*, and *Trochilidæ*. <Ann. Lyc. Nat. Hist., N. Y., VIII, pp. 404–405. Description of *Amazilia graysoni.*

1871. GRAYSON, ANDREW JACKSON. On the Physical Geography and Natural History of the Islands of the Tres Marias and Socorro off the Western Coast of Mexico. Edited by Geo. N. Lawrence. <Proc. Bost. Soc. Nat. Hist., XIV, pp. 261–302. In addition to Grayson's notes, Lawrence gives a few remarks on certain birds said to have been taken on the Tres Marias by Xantus and describes *Pyrrhophæna graysoni* (=*Amazilia graysoni*) and *Sterna fuliginosa crissalis* (ex Baird MSS.).

1871. LAWRENCE, GEORGE N. Descriptions of New Species of Birds from Mexico, Central America, and South America, with a note on *Rallus longirostris*. <Ann. Lyc. Nat. Hist. N. Y., X, pp. 1–21. Description of *Parula insularis* (=*Compsothlypis insularis*).

1874. BAIRD, SPENCER F. <History of North American Birds, II, pp. 515, 516. Description of *Dryobates scalaris graysoni.*

1874. LAWRENCE, GEORGE N. Birds of Western and Northwestern Mexico. <Mem. Bost. Soc. Nat. Hist. II, pp. 265–319. Contains extracts from Grayson's notes on various species of birds of the Tres Marias.

1876. WALLACE, ALFRED RUSSELL. Geographical Distribution of Animals, II, pp. 59–60. Summary of the fauna of the Tres Marias, comprising 52 species of birds, 3 mammals, and several species of snakes and lizards.

1877. ALLEN, JOEL ASAPH. <Mon. N. Am. Rodentia, 347–348. Description of *Lepus graysoni.*

1877–79. GRAYSON, ANDREW JACKSON. Historia Natural de las Islas de las Tres Marias y Socorro. <La Naturaleza IV, pp. 159, 203, and 252. A Spanish translation, by Señor Don Aniceto Moreno, of Colonel Grayson's paper originally published in the Annals of the Lyceum of Natural History, New York, X, 1871.

1878. RIDGWAY, ROBERT. Description of a New Wren from the Tres Marias Islands. <Bull. Nutt. Orn. Club, III, p. 10. *Thryothorus felix lawrencii* (= *T. lawrencii*).

1879–82. ALSTON, EDWARD R. <Biologia Centrali-Americana. Mammalia. 1879–1882. Notes on *Vesperugo parvulus* (= *Rhogeësa parvula*), p. 21, *Lepus graysoni*, p. 177, and a seal, p. 210, on the Tres Marias.

1879–98. SALVIN, OSBERT, and GODMAN, F. DuCane. <Biologia Centrali-Americana' Aves I and II, 1879–1898. Contains notes on various species of birds of the Tres Marias, based on the work of Grayson and Forrer.

1880. ALLEN, JOEL ASAPH. History of North American Pinnipeds, 1880, p. 290. Misc. publication No. 12, U. S. Geol. and Geog. Survey Terr. Quotation of Dampier's notes on seals about the Tres Marias.

1882. RIDGWAY, ROBERT. Description of Several New Races of American Birds. <Proc. U. S. Nat. Mus., V, p. 12, 1882. Description of *Merula flavirostris graysoni*.

1882. STEJNEGER, LEONHARD. Description of Two New Races of *Myadestes obscurus* Lafr. <Proc. U. S. Nat. Mus., IV, p. 373, 1882. Description of *Myadestes obscurus insularis*.

1882. THOMAS, OLDFIELD. Biologia Centrali-Americana, Mammalia, Supplement, 1882. Notes on various species of mammals found on the Tres Marias: *Vesperugo parvulus*, p. 203; *Atalapha noveboracensis*, p. 205; *Vespertilio nigricans*, p. 206; *Macrotus waterhousii*, p. 207; *Charonycteris mexicana* [= *Glossophaga mutica*], p. 207; *Procyon cancrivorus*, p. 208; *Lepus graysoni*, p. 211.

1885. MADARÁSZ, JULIUS VON. Ornithologiai Közlemények A Magyar Nemzeti Muzeum Gyüjteményéböl. <Természetrajzi Füzetek, IX, p. 74, Feb. 20, 1885. Description of *Vireo forreri*.

1887. RIDGWAY, ROBERT. <Manual of North American Birds, 1887. Descriptions of *Iache lawrencei* (ex Berlepsch MS.), p. 320; *Platypsaris insularis*, p. 325; *Piranga flammea*, p. 457.

1887. RIDGWAY, ROBERT. A Review of the Genus *Psittacula* of Brisson. <Proc. U. S. Nat. Museum, X, 541, 1887. Description of *Psittacula insularis*.

1891. BRYANT, WALTER E. Andrew Jackson Grayson. <Zoe, II, pp. 34–68, 1891. A short account of Grayson's life, with extracts from his journals on the habits of certain birds of the Tres Marias.

1898. EVERMANN, BARTON WARREN. Notes on Fishes Collected by E. W. Nelson on the Tres Marias Islands and in Sinaloa and Jalisco, Mexico. < Proc. Biol. Soc., Washington, XII, pp. 1–3, 1898. Records *Agonostomus nasutus* Günth. on Maria Magdalena and Maria Cleofa.

1898. MERRIAM, C. HART. Mammals of Tres Marias Islands off Western Mexico. <Proc. Biol. Soc. Washington, XII, pp. 13–19, 1898. Descriptions of *Marmosa insularis*, *Oryzomys nelsoni*, *Peromyscus madrensis*, *Procyon lotor insularis*, *Glossophaga mutica*, with notes on other species of mammals occurring on the islands.

1898. NELSON, EDWARD WILLIAM. Descriptions of New Birds from the Tres Marias Islands, Western Mexico. <Proc. Biol. Soc. Washington, XII, pp. 5–11, 1898. Descriptions of the following new species and subspecies: *Columba flavirostris madrensis*, *Leptotila capitalis*, *Buteo borealis fumosus*, *Polyborus cheriway pallidus*, *Trogon ambiguus goldmani*, *Nyctidromus albicollis insularis*, *Myiopagis placens minimus*, *Cardinalis cardinalis mariæ*, *Vireo hypochryseus sordidus*, *Melanotis cærulescens longirostris*, *Thryothorus lawrencii magdalenæ*.

1898. GREENMAN, JESSE M. Diagnoses of New and Critical Mexican Phanerogams. <Proc. Am. Acad. Arts and Sci., XXXIII, No. 25, pp. 471–489, June, 1898. <Descriptions of *Ægiphila pacifica*, *Beloperone nelsoni*, *Buxus pubescens*, and *Cordia insularis*.

1898. MILLSPAUGH, CHARLES F. Notes and New Species of the Genus Euphorbia. <Botanical Gazette, XXVI, pp. 265–270, Oct., 1898. Descriptions of *Euphorbia nelsoni* and *Euphorbia subcærulea tresmariæ*.

[Names of new species in black-face type.]

Abutilon reventum, 79.
Acacia, 83.
Acalypha, 90.
Actitis macularia, 34.
Adiantum tenerum, 91.
Ægialitis semipalmata, 34.
Ægiphila pacifica, 13, 78, 87-88.
Agave, 9, 12, 90-91.
Agkistrodon bilineatus, 71.
Agonostomus nasutus, 11.
Albizzia occidentalis, 83.
Amazilia cinnamomica, 45-46.
  graysoni, 12, 22, 45, 46.
Amazona finschi, 41.
  ♀ oratrix, 39-41.
Amyris, 80.
Anolis nebulosus, **65**.
Anous stolidus, 26.
  stolidus ridgwayi, 26-27.
Antigonon leptopus, 88.
Arctocephalus townsendi, 18.
Ardea candidissima, 33.
  egretta, **33**.
  herodias, 33.
Argemone ochroleuca, 78.
Aristolochia pardina, 88.
Arundo donax, 91.
Aspidium patens, **91**.
  trifoliatum, 91.
Astragalinus psaltria mexicanus, 52.
Ateleia, 82.
Awaous, 11.
Baccharis glutinosa, 84.
Bascanion lineatum, 70.
Bassovia donnell-smithii, 89.
Bat, Big-eared, 18.
  Maximilian's Black, 15, 18.
  Mexican Red, 19.
Batis maritima, 88.
Bauhinia, 83.
Beloperone comosa, 86, 87.
  nelsoni, 13, 78, 86-87.
Bignonia æquinoctialis, 86.
  sarmentosa, 86.
Bithynis jamaicensis, 74-75.
  vollenhovenii, 75.
Boa imperator, 63, 69.
Booby, Blue-footed, 31-32.
  Brewster's, 29, 30.
  Webster's, 29.
Brachyrhamphus brevirostris, 23.
  hypoleucus, 23.
Roddlia verticillata, 84.
Bursera gummifera, 80.
Buteo borealis calurus, 37.
  borealis fumosus, 12, 37-38.
  borealis montana, 37.
  borealis socorroensis, 37-38.
Boxus pubescens, 13, 78, 90.
Campephilus, 23.
Canavalia gladiata, **82**.
Capparis breynia, 78.
  cynophallophora, **78**.
Capraria biflora, 86.
Caracara, Tres Marias, 38-39.
Cardinalis cardinalis mariæ, 12, 22, 52.
  virginianus, 52.
  virginianus igneus, 52.
Cardinal, Tres Marias, 52.
Cardiospermum corindum, 81.

Casearia, 83.
  corymbosa, 83.
  sylvestris, 83.
Cassia, 12.
  atomaria, **82**.
  biflora, 82.
  emarginata, 82.
Cathartes aura, 37.
Celtis monoica, 90.
Cereus, 12, 51.
Ceryle alcyon, 43.
Chlorostilbon insularis, 62.
  pucherani, 62.
Chœronycteris mexicana, 19.
Chordeiles actipennis texensis, 45.
Chrysotis levaillantii, 39.
Ciccaba squamulata, 39.
Circe latirostris, 46.
Cissampelos pareira, **78**.
Cissolopha, 23.
  beecheyi, 50.
Cissus sicyoides, 80.
Citharexylum affinis, 87.
Cnemidophorus gularis mexicanus, 63, **68**.
  mariarum, 12, 63, 67-68.
Coccoloba leptostachya, 88.
Coccyzus minor, **42**.
Colubrina arborea, 80.
Columba flavirostris, 35.
  flavirostris madrensis, 12, 22, 35.
Columbigallina passerina pallescens, **37**.
Compsothlypis inornata, 55.
  insularis, 11, **12**, 22, 55-56.
  nigrilora, 55.
  pitiayumi, 55.
  pulchra, 55, 56.
Conocarpus erectus, 83.
Contopus richardsoni, **49**.
Conurus, 23.
Conyza lyrata, 84.
Cordia insularis, 13, **78**, **85**.
  sonoræ, 85.
Cormorant, 32.
Corvus mexicanus, 50.
Crataeva tapia, 78.
Crocodile, 11.
Crocodylus americanus, **64**.
Crotalus, 71.
Crotolaria lupulina, 81.
Croton ciliato-glandulosus, 90.
Crow, Mexican, 50.
Ctenosaura teres, 65-66.
Cuckoo, Mangrove, 42.
Cyanospiza, 23.
Cyperus incompletus, 91.
  ligularis, 91.
Dactyloctenium ægyptiacum, 91.
Datura discolor, 86.
Dendroica æstiva rubiginosa, 56.
  æstiva morcomi, 56.
  auduboni, 56.
  townsendii, 56.
Desmodium, 81.
Diplotropis diplotropis, 63, 69.
Dove, Mexican Ground, 37.
  Mourning, 36.
  Tres Marias, 36.
  White-fronted, 36.
  White-winged, 36-37.
Drymarchon corais melanurus, 70

96 INDEX.

Drymobius boddærti, 69–70.
Dryobates scalaris, 43.
  scalaris bairdi, 43.
  scalaris graysoni, 12, 23, 43–44.
  scalaris lucasanus, 43.
  scalaris sinaloensis, 43–44.
Egret, American, 33.
Elainea placens, 50.
Eleusine indica, 91.
Empidonax difficilis, 49.
Erythrina lanata, 13, 78, 81.
Eupatorium, 84.
  collinum, 84.
Euphorbia, 12, 88, 89.
  nelsoni, 13, 78, 89–90.
  subcœrulea tresmariæ, 13, 78, 88–89.
Falco albigularis, 38.
  columbarius, 38.
  peregrinus anatum, 38.
  peregrinus nigriceps, 38.
  sparverius, 38.
Falcon, White-throated, 38.
Ficus fasciculata, 90.
  radulina, 90.
Florisuga mellivora, 62.
Flycatcher, Arizona Crested, 48.
  Beardless, 49.
  Golden Crowned, 50.
  Little Golden Crowned, 50.
  Olivaceous, 48–49.
  Western, 49.
Fregata aquila, 33.
Garcia nutans, 90.
Gecarcinus digueti, 73–74.
Gilibertia insularis, 13, 78, 83–84.
Glandina turris, 11.
Glossophaga mutica, 11, 18–19.
Glossophaga, Tres Marias, 18–19.
Goldfinch, Mexican, 52.
Gonolobus, 84.
Grackle, Great-tailed, 52.
Granatellus francescæ, 12, 22, 56–57.
  venustus, 57.
Grapsus grapsus, 74.
Guaiacum coulteri, 79.
Guarea, 80.
Guazuma ulmifolia, 79.
Gull, American herring, 23.
  Heermann's, 23–24.
Gymnogramme calomelanos, 91.
Hadrostomus aglaiæ affinis, 47.
Hæmatopus frazari 34–35,
  galapagensis, 34–35,
  palliatus, 34 35.
Haliplana fuliginosa crissalis, 24.
Hawk, Duck, 38.
  Pigeon, 38.
  Sparrow, 38.
  Tres Marias Red-tailed, 37, 38.
Heliotropium curassavicum, 85.
  indicum, 85.
Heron, Great Blue, 33.
  Snowy, 33,
  Yellow-crowned Night, 33, 34.
Heteropterys floribunda, 79.
Hibiscus tiliaceus, 79.
Hippocratea, 80.
Hirundo erythrogaster, 54.
Humming Bird, Grayson's, 45, 46.
  Lawrence's, 46, 47.
Hylocichla ustulata, 60.
  ustulata almæ, 60.
  ustulata swainsoni, 60.
Hypotriorchis rufigularis, 38.
Hyptis albida, 88.
Iache latirostris, 46, 47.
  lawrencei, 12, 22, 46.
Icterus graysoni, 12, 22, 50–51.
  pustulatus, 51.
Iguana, Black, 65, 66.
Ipomœa, 12.
  bona-nox, 85.
  pedunicularis, 85.
Iresine interrupta, 88.
Jacquemontia violacea, 86.
Jacquinia macrocarpa, 84.
Jay, Beechey's, 52.
Kingbird, Couch's, 48.
Kingfisher, Belted, 43.

Kinosternon integrum, 64.
Lamellaxis, 11.
Lampropeltis micropholis oligozona, 70.
Lantana horrida, 87.
Larus argentatus smithsonianus, 23.
  heermanni, 23–24.
Lasiurus borealis mexicana, 15, 19.
Leptophis diplotropis, 69.
Leptotila albifrons, 36,
  capitalis, 12, 22, 36.
  fulviventris brachyptera, 36.
Lepus graysoni, 11, 16–17.
Lonchocarpus, 82.
Lovebird, Tres Marias, 41–42.
Man-o'-war bird, 33.
Marmosa insularis, 11, 15–16.
Melanerpes, 23.
Melanotis cærulescens, 59.
  cærulescens longirostris, 12, 22, 59.
  hypoleucus, 59.
Melochia tomentosa, 79.
Melopelia leucoptera, 22, 36–37.
Merula flavirostris, 60, 61.
  grayi, 62.
  graysoni, 12, 22, 60–62.
  tristis, 62.
Micropallas, 39.
Mikania cordifolia, 84.
Mimus polyglottos, 57.
Mockingbird, 57.
Momotus, 23.
Mouse, Tres Marias, 16.
Murrelet, Short-billed, 23.
Mus rattus, 16.
Myadestes obscurus, 58.
  obscurus insularis, 12, 22, 59–60.
  obscurus occidentalis, 60.
Myiarchus lawrencei olivascens, 48–49,
  mexicanus magister, 48.
Myiopagis placens, 50.
  placens minimus, 12, 22, 50.
Myiozetetes, 23.
Myotis nigricans, 15, 18.
Myriocarpa longipes, 90.
Nicotiana trigonophylla, 86.
Nighthawk, Texas, 45.
Nycticorax violaceus, 33–34.
Nyctidromus albicollis, 44.
  albicollis insularis, 12, 22, 44.
  albicollis merrilli, 44.
Oceanodroma melania, 28.
Ochna, 80.
Ocypoda, 74.
Ocypode kuhlii, 74.
  occidentalis, 74.
Opeas subula, 11.
Opossum, Tres Marias Pigmy, 11, 15–16.
Opuntia, 12, 83.
Oriole, Grayson's, 50.
Ornithion imberbe, 22, 49.
  imberbe ridgwayi, 49.
Orthalicus undatus, 11.
  undatus melanocheilus, 11.
Oryzomys nelsoni, 11, 16.
Osprey, 39.
Otopterus mexicanus, 18.
Owl, Barn, 39.
  Burrowing, 39.
Oxybelis acuminatus, 69.
Oyster-catcher, American, 34–35.
Pandion haliætus carolinensis, 39.
Panicum brevifolium, 91.
Parauque, Tres Marias, 44.
Parrot, Double yellow-head, 39–41.
Parthenium hysterophorus, 84.
Parula insularis, 55.
  Tres Marias, 55.
Passiflora, 12, 83.
Paullinia sessiliflora, 81.
Pelecanus californicus, 32–33.
Pelican, California Brown, 32–33.
Petasophora thalassina, 62.
Perityle microglossa, 84.
Peromyscus madrensis, 11, 16.
Petrel, Black, 28.
Phaëthon æthereus, 28–29.
Phalacrocorax, 32.
Phaseolus, 82.
Phocæna communis, 19.

Phyllodactylus tuberculosus, 63, 64-65.
Physalis pubescens, 86.
Phytolacca octandra, 88.
Playa, 23.
Picramnia, 80.
ciliata, 80
Picus scalaris graysoni, 43.
Pigeon, Tres Marias, 35.
Pilocarpus insularis, 13, 78, 80.
Piper aduncum, 88.
Pipile, 23.
Piranga bidentata, 53, 54.
bidentata flammea, 12, 22, 52, 53, 54
ludoviciana, 23, 52.
Pithecolobium, 12.
dulce, 39, 77, 83.
ligustrinum, 83.
Platypsaris aglaiæ, 47-48.
aglaiæ albiventris, 47, 48.
aglaiæ insularis, 12, 22, 47-48.
aglaiæ anmichrasti, 47-48.
Plover, Semipalmated, 34.
Pluchea odorata, 84.
Polyborus audubonii, 38.
audubonii insularis, 22.
cheriway pallidus, 12, 22, 38-39.
Polygyra ventroanla, 11.
Porophyllum nummularium, 84.
Porpoise, Common, 19.
Long-nosed, 19.
Portlandia pterosperma, 84.
Procyon lotor insularis, 11, 17.
Prodelphinus longirostris, 19.
Psidium, 35, 83.
Psittacula cyanopyga, 41-42.
insularis, 12, 22, 41-42.
Pteris longifolia, 91.
Puffinus cuneatus, 27-28.
knudseni, 27.
Pyrgisoma, 23.
Pyrrhophæna graysoni, 45.
Raccoon, Tres Marias, 17.
Rat, Black, 16.
Nelson's Rice, 16.
Rhogeëssa parvula, 11, 18.
Rhogeëssa, Tres Marias, 18.
Rhynchosia minima, 82.
precatoria, 82.
Russelia sarmentosa, 85.
Quiscalus macrourus, 52.
Saltator, 23.
Salvia aliena, 88.
Sandpiper, Spotted, 34.
Sceloporus boulengeri, 67.
clarkii, 67.
horridus, 67.
oligoporus, 67.
Schœpfia schreberi, 80.
Sea Lion, 15, 17-18.
Serjania mexicana, 80.
Shearwater, Wedge-tailed, 27-28.
Solanum, 12.
callicarpæfolium, 86.
lanceæfolium, 86.
nigrum, 86.
torvum, 86.
verbascifolium, 86.
Solitaire, Tres Marias, 59-60.
Spanish cedar, 7, 8, 9, 12.
Speotyto cunicularia hypogæa, 39.
Stachys coccinea, 88.
Stegnosperma halimifolia, 88.
Sterna elegans, 24.
fuliginosa crissalis, 24-26.
galericulata, 24.
maxima, 24.
Strix pratincola, 39.
Sula bassana, 29.
brewsteri, 29-30.
gossi, 31, 32.

Sula nebouxii, 31-32.
piscator, 31.
websteri, 29.
Swallow, Barn, 54.
Tanager, Louisiana, 52.
Tres Marias, 52, 53.
Tephrosia, 81.
Tern, Elegant, 24.
Pacific Noddy, 26-27.
Pacific Sooty, 24-26.
Royal, 24.
Ternstrœmia maltbya, 12, 78.
Thalurania glaucopis, 62.
luciæ, 62.
Thrush, Olive-backed, 60.
Russet-backed, 60.
Thryothorus felix, 22, 57, 58.
lawrencii, 12, 22, 57, 58.
lawrencii magdalenæ, 12, 22, 58
Tournefortia candida, 85.
cymosa, 85.
velutina, 85.
Totanus flavipes, 34.
Tres Marias, Blue Mockingbird, 59.
Caracara, 38-39.
Cardinal, 52.
Chat-Warbler, 56-57.
Cottontail, 16-17.
Dove, 36.
Glossophaga, 18-19.
Lovebird, 41-42.
Mouse, 16.
Parauque, 44.
Parula, 55-56.
Pigeon, 35.
Pigmy Opossum, 11, 15-16.
Raccoon, 17.
Red-tailed Hawk, 37-38.
Rhogeëssa, 18.
Robin, 60-61.
Solitaire, 59-60.
Tanager, 52.
Vireo, 54-55.
Trichilia spondioides, 80.
Trixis frutescens, 84.
Trogon ambiguus, 42.
ambiguus goldmani, 12, 22, 42-43.
Trogon, Goldman's, 42-43.
Tropic Bird, Red-billed, 28-29.
Turdus flavirostris, 60.
Turtle, Mud, 11.
Tyrannus melancholicus couchi, 22, 48.
Urauomitra guatemalensis, 62.
Urvillea ulmacea, 81.
Uta lateralis, 66-67.
Vireo flavoviridis forreri, 12, 21, 22, 54, 55.
hypochryseus, 54.
hypochryseus sordidus, 12, 22, 54-55.
Vireo, Forrer's, 54.
Tres Marias, 54-55.
Vulture, Turkey, 37.
Warbler, Alaskan Yellow, 56.
Audubon's, 56.
Pileolated, 57.
Townsend's, 56.
Tres Marias Chat-, 56, 57.
Western Yellow, 56.
Wilsonia pusilla pileolata, 57.
Wissadula hirsutiflora, 79.
Wood Pewee, Western, 49.
Wren, Magdalena, 58.
Maria Madre, 57-58.
Ximenia americana, 80.
Yellow-legs, 34.
Zalophus californianus, 17-18.
Zamia loddigesii, 91.
Zanthoxylum insularis, 13, 78, 79.
nelsoni, 13, 78, 79.
Zenaidura macroura, 36.

www.ingramcontent.com/pod-product-compliance
Lightning Source LLC
Chambersburg PA
CBHW032245080426
42735CB00008B/1013